Building integrated photovoltaics/
a handbook

Building integrated photovoltaics/ a handbook

Simon Roberts & Nicolò Guariento

Birkhäuser
Basel · Boston · Berlin

Content

1. INTRODUCTION

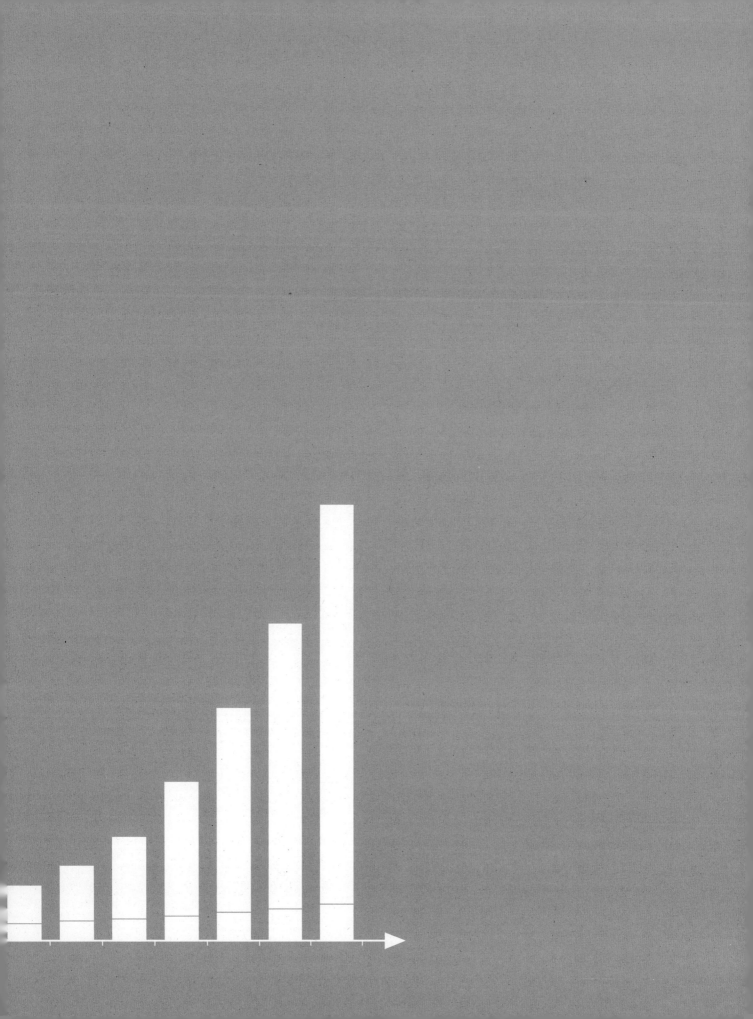

1.1 Handbook coverage

This handbook is aimed at architects and designers. Its main objective is to address PV technology as one more building-cladding option from an architect's point of view. Most examples here are of new buildings, but the guidance is equally relevant for renovation of existing buildings.

Part 1 covers the basic principles:
— Chapter 2 is an introduction to PV technology.
— Chapter 3 examines the main PV issues for building designers.
— Chapter 4 deals with the building envelope as a support for PV.

Part 2 consisting of Chapters 5 to 10 forms the core of the handbook. These chapters present in further detail the design integration of PV modules in the main façade systems together with case-study projects in each chapter. The specific façade systems and building elements covered are:
— Shading systems
— Rainscreen systems
— Stick system curtain walls
— Unitised curtain wall
— Double-skin façades
— Atria and canopies

Part 3 briefly covers specific issues of BIPV in the residential sector and refurbishment applications.

Finally Part 4 draws some of the information together: Chapter 13 collates statistics from all the case studies and Chapter 14 is a glossary of terms, both for PV technology and façade engineering.

1.2 Further reading

Though not covered in this handbook, we take for granted that PV should be considered as an integral part of a broad strategy of energy-efficient building design. The aim is to convert the buildings from energy consumers into energy producers, and this cannot be achieved with PV alone.
Also not covered here are cost implications, subsidies, feed-in tariffs or carbon pricing since these are locally dependent and rapidly changing.
We only mention roof systems briefly since the literature and examples of PV integration in standard roofs is available through many sources and there are an increasing number of proprietary roof tile systems coming onto the market.

Fig. 1.1 The Kesch hut (Albula Alps, CH) with a 2.7 kW$_P$ PV array on the roof and south façade, as an example of an off-grid stand-alone PV installation.
Photo: Toni Spirig

Fig. 1.2 The 14 MW$_P$ PV installation at Nellis Air Force Base (USA) with tracking modules, as an example of a solar farm.
Photo courtesy: U.S. Air Force

1.3 Photovoltaic installations

Solar electricity using photovoltaic (PV) technology is the direct generation of electricity from sunlight. PV modules work silently with no moving parts, minimal maintenance and no pollutant emissions.

PV is one of the fastest growing sectors of the renewable energy industry. The market is driven by concerns about environmental awareness of climate-change mitigation and local air quality, as well as national energy security issues and the rising cost of fossil fuels. The start of the 21st century has seen an accelerating take-up of PV installation in many countries (**Fig. 1.3** for the member countries of the International Energy Agency or IEA).

There are several types of PV installation which include:
— off-grid (stand alone) with battery storage (**Fig. 1.1**)
— grid-connected ground-mounted, such as a solar farm (**Fig. 1.2**)
— grid-connected roof-mounted, mostly by lay-on technology (**1.5**)
— grid-connected building-integrated (**Fig. 1.4**)

Both roof-mounted and building-integrated PV installations are usually grid-connected providing local, embedded generation. This means the generation capacity is sited amongst the buildings using the power, in contrast to central generation by large power stations that are linked to users via long, high-voltage transmission lines.

There are many reasons to encourage local generation of energy:
— Supplying a portion of the annual electrical requirement of the building reduces energy costs for the owners.
— The energy generation is next to where it is consumed and electricity distribution losses are reduced compared to central generation.
— There is space on roofs and façades that can be utilised for energy generation.
— Using renewable energy makes a contribution to the environmental agenda.
— Having the generation means close to building users raises awareness of energy in general and helps encourage energy efficiency by users.

Fig. 1.3 Cumulative installed PV capacity in the reporting countries to the IEA PVPS Programme for the years 1992 to 2007. The PV capacity is made up of grid-connected and off-grid (stand alone) installations. The addition for 2007 was 2300 MW$_P$, a growth of 40% from 2006.
Source: www.iea-pups.org

Fig. 1.4 Entrance to the Solar Office at Doxford International Business Park (UK), 73 kW$_P$ PV array, as an example of a building-integrated PV installation.
Photo courtesy: Schüco International KG

Fig. 1.5 20 kW$_P$ array on the roof of an office building in Berlin (D), as an example of a roof-mounted PV installation.
Photo courtesy: Schüco International KG

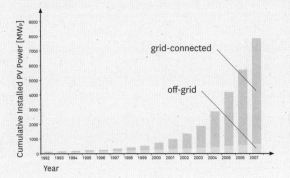

1.4 Building integrated PV

In a lay-on or additive solution, PV modules are secured to a roof or onto a façade using a metal structure. The PV system is an additional structural element with the sole function of generating energy.

In contrast, building-integrated PV (BIPV), the subject of this handbook, refers to the application of PV in which the system, as well as having the function of producing electricity, also takes on the role of a building element.

BIPV has a low penetration in the overall PV market. For example, the proportions by generation capacity for Germany in 2004 were 70% ground mounted and 29% roof mounted with BIPV at only 1%. Nevertheless PV technology is mature and the cost/performance balance is steadily improving. Integration into buildings should be encouraged beyond just demonstration or educational projects.

One aspect still to address is dissemination of PV design possibilities within design teams. Through this handbook we aim to present PV, not as an alien technology, but as an alternative to metal cladding or standard curtain walling. Our goal is to help designers to consider PV modules as an attractive alternative to other cladding materials, with its particular image and requirements.

More than just providing electrical energy, BIPV can enhance and satisfy a building image. BIPV makes a statement about innovative architectural as well as engineering design.

Fig. 1.6 Integration of PV into the glazed roof of the Mont-Cenis Academy in Herne (D).
Photo: Monika Nikolic/arturimages

1.5 BIPV for designers

This handbook supports the notion that design with BIPV should aspire to have high architectural quality **(Fig. 1.6)**. The criteria for achieving this quality is defined by the Photovoltaic Power Systems Programme of the IEA as "natural integration of PV systems, PV systems that are architecturally pleasing within the context of the building, good material and colour composition, PV systems that adapt well to overall modularity, the visual aspect of the grid which is in harmony with the building and creates a satisfactory composition, PV systems that are appropriate to the context of the building and the integration of which is well designed, use of PV that has generated an innovative concept."

The design team will need to judge exposure of the PV integration. There is a scale of design approaches:
— PV can be out of sight, for instance high on a roof. This may be appropriate for a conservation area or historic building, or where the absolute maximum collection efficiency is needed.
— PV can be a small positive addition, such as on shading devices over widows.
— PV can be integrated into a vertical façade in a discreet fashion without changing the building's image.
— PV can be a leading part of the design process determining the overall building appearance and form.

2. PV BASICS

Fig. 2.1 An array of polycrystalline silicon modules integrated into a sloped wall.
Photo courtesy: Schüco International KG

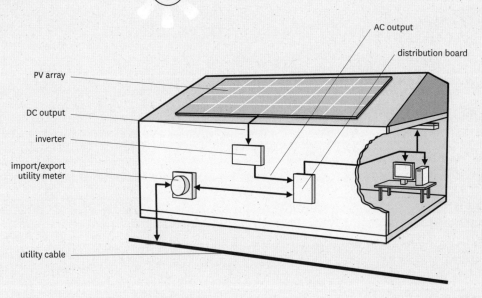

Fig. 2.2 Basic parts of a grid-connected BIPV system showing the direction of flow of electrical energy. The PV output can help power loads within the building. When there is excess output, this energy flows back onto the utility cable.

2.1 PV system overview

PV systems work by converting sunlight directly into electricity. The conversion process takes place in a solar or PV cell, usually made of silicon, although new materials are being developed. PV cells need to be encapsulated and are connected as a group into a larger DC electrical unit called a module (also known as a PV panel). A group of modules is referred to as a PV array. To capture the maximum of sunlight, PV arrays are designed for outdoor use and need to be durable (Fig. 2.1).

In this handbook we refer only to PV systems connected to the local electricity distribution grid through a PV inverter (Fig. 2.2), and not to stand-alone systems that charge batteries. PV inverters connected to the grid create an AC output that is in phase with the grid-supplied AC. PV inverters are designed to shut down automatically upon loss of grid supply, for safety reasons. All the parts separate from the PV modules themselves are called the balance-of-system (BOS).

Grid-connected PV systems can supply electricity for use in the building where they are mounted. When demand from building loads is high, all the PV output is used, so reducing grid consumption and the utility bill. When building demand is low, electricity is exported onto the grid. The switch between building use or export happens automatically without any human intervention. Utility companies in different countries have various arrangements for paying the owner for electricity produced. This ranges from a low price related to the commercial rate for conventional power to what is known as a feed-in tariff which compensates over a number of years for the original cost of the PV installation.

This chapter goes into the details of types of PV cells and PV modules relevant to building integration:
— 2.2 PV materials and cells
— 2.3 PV modules
— 2.4 Module options
— 2.5 Module specification and STC

2.2 PV materials and cells
2.2.1 The photoelectric process

The PV process works by the photovoltaic effect in semiconductor materials. When light strikes the cell, a portion of it is absorbed within the semiconductor material and "knocks" electrons loose, enabling an electrical charge to flow freely within the material (Fig. 2.4. PV cells have an in-built electric field that acts to force electrons, freed by light absorption, to flow in a certain direction. The field is created by doping (controlled introduction of impurities) in silicon with elements such as phosphorus or boron to create n-type or p-type zones.

By placing metal contacts on the top and bottom of the PV cell, the current generated can be put to work by passing through an external circuit. The current is generated silently with no moving parts, no emissions and the cells need no maintenance, apart from keeping the top surface of the module clean for the passage of light.

In a graph of the spectrum (Fig. 2.3), the visible part corresponds to the wavelength range, 400–700 nm. The overall curve in the figure shows the solar spectrum stretching into the infra-red beyond 2000 nm. Silicon PV cells absorb most of the visible spectrum and the near infra-red up to 1100 nm.

Since practical efficiencies are in the range of 5–20%, 80% or more of the incident light energy is converted into heat (Fig. 2.5). The active PV materials of PV cells can be classified as either of:
— crystalline where they are sliced from ingots or castings or grown as thin slices from ribbons
— thin film where they are deposited as a thin layer on a low cost backing

In 2006, 95% of the world PV market was crystalline silicon.

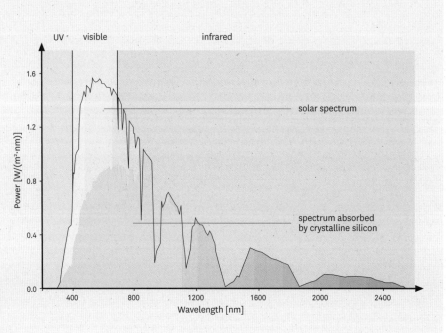

Fig. 2.3 Comparative spectra for solar input (including atmospheric losses) and the spectral parts absorbed by crystalline silicon PV cells.
(The solar spectrum is AM 1.5 at an irradiance of 1000 W/m².)

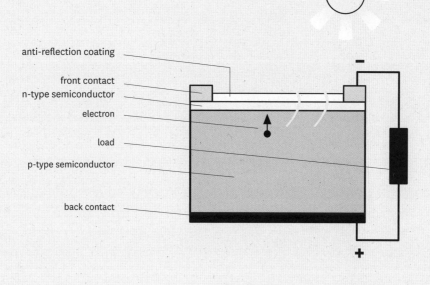

anti-reflection coating

front contact
n-type semiconductor

electron

load

p-type semiconductor

back contact

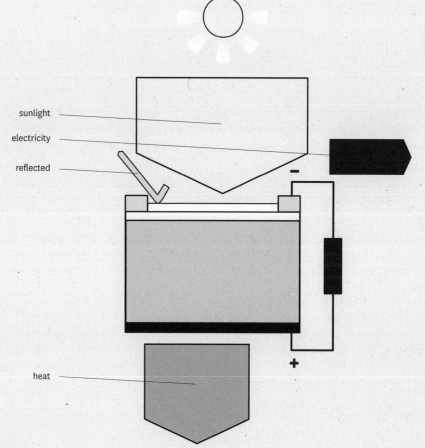

sunlight

electricity

reflected

heat

Fig. 2.4 Schematic of a single PV cell showing the main functional parts for conversion of light to electrical energy. The thickness of the absorbing layer is exaggerated to show an electron carrier.

Fig. 2.5 Schematic of principal energy flows of a solar cell emphasising that a significant proportion of the energy is absorbed as heat.

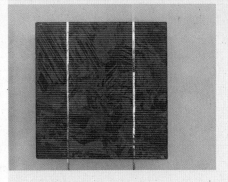

Fig. 2.6 The G8 "solar showcase" BIPV pavilion built in 1998. This close-up shows the outline of monocrystalline cells within the modules.
Photo: Christian Richters

Fig. 2.7 An individual polycrystalline silicon cell showing clearly two busbars. This cell is from the rainscreen case study in Chapter 6.
Photo: Frank P. Palmer
Courtesy: Simone Giostra & Partners/Arup

2.2.2 Monocrystalline silicon

Monocrystalline (also known as single crystal) silicon cells are usually manufactured from a single crystal ingot of high purity, most commonly grown by the Czochralski method (crucible drawing process). The diameters are 12.5 or 15 cm (4 or 5 inches). The ingot is cut into thin slices which are processed to make PV cells.
The circular shape is cut away for better packing into a module. Depending on how much of the monocrystal is removed, the range of cell shapes produced can be round, semi-round or square (Fig. 2.6).

Other methods for making monocrystalline silicon are edge-defined film-fed growth (EFG) and string ribbon processes. These can be grown at the right thickness, so avoiding the slicing process and losses. Also they can be cut square with right-angle corners and no loss of material.

To increase the amount of light absorbed into the cell, which will result in higher currents, a thin anti-reflection (AR) coating is applied as either silicon nitride or titanium oxide. This makes the appearance dark blue. An option for effect, perhaps in a BIPV façade, is to leave off the AR coating altogether leaving the cells a natural dark grey, although reflection losses increase from 3% to 30%. Other AR coatings can give a range of colours other than dark blue, but the efficiency is reduced by a few percent. PV modules made with these cells would be special custom-made products.

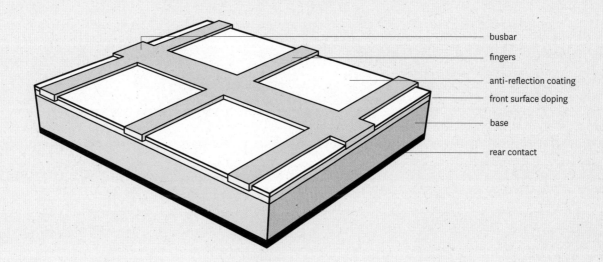

busbar

fingers

anti-reflection coating

front surface doping

base

rear contact

The basic design of a crystalline silicon cell is shown in **Fig. 2.8**. The thickness of the substrate is 200–400 µm (0.2–0.4 mm) while the depth of the front surface doping layer is less than 1 µm. On the front side, a metallisation grid consists of fingers to conduct the generated current to central collectors or busbars. The selected metallisation pattern is a compromise between shadow losses that block light and resistance losses that reduce electrical output.

The back contact can be applied over more of the surface. A full-surface aluminium coating is printed and processed to help the cell efficiency. When cells are fabricated into glass-glass laminates, the shiny back face is visible inside the building.

2.2.3 Polycrystalline silicon

An alternative way of making silicon PV cells is from polycrystalline silicon (also known as multicrystalline silicon). The starting material is melted and cast in a cuboid form. As the silicon solidifies, large crystals are formed with grain sizes from a few millimetres to a few centimetres. The grain boundaries reduce the efficiency slightly.
The ingot is cut into bars and then sliced into thin wafers that are used to make the cells, similar to the completion of single crystal cells **(Fig. 2.7)**.
Polycrystalline silicon is slightly less expensive than monocrystalline silicon but also slightly less efficient. There is a trend to larger cells of 21 × 21 cm (8 inch square) for lower costs and higher overall module efficiency.

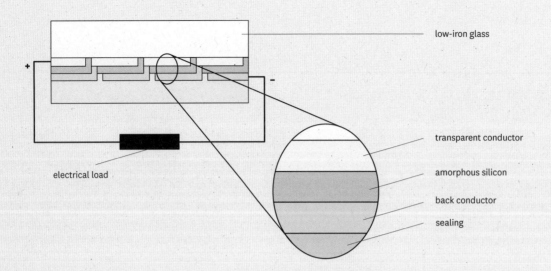

Fig. 2.9 Schematic cross section of a thin-film silicon module of four cells. The thickness of the active layers has been exaggerated to show how the electrical connection between adjacent cells is formed.

low-iron glass

electrical load

transparent conductor

amorphous silicon

back conductor

sealing

2.2.4 Thin-film technologies

Thin-film cells are constructed by depositing extremely thin layers of PV materials onto a superstrate, the front glass, or onto a substrate, the module backside. Connections between the cells are an integral part of the cell fabrication so the PV module is made at the same time. Amorphous silicon, copper indium diselenide (CIS) and cadmium telluride (CdTe) are used as the active semiconductor materials. Compared to manufacturing temperatures of up to 1500°C for crystalline silicon cells, thin-film cells require deposition temperatures of between 200°C and 600°C. The lower material and energy consumption and capability for high automation of module production offer considerable cost savings. However the efficiency is lower than for crystalline silicon technology. The lower efficiency means that a larger area is required to achieve the desired power.

Fig. 2.9 shows the build-up of layers for amorphous silicon as the active thin film. A transparent conductive oxide (TCO) layer, such as tin oxide, is first applied. The individual cells are formed by scribing through the TCO layer into parallel stripes. The next layers are applied in strips and offset in order to achieve the inter-cell connections.

CdTe thin-film modules are made in a similar way to amorphous silicon onto a glass superstrate. CdTe modules have the lowest production costs among the current thin-film technologies. Although cadmium is a heavy metal with environmental issues, the chemical form as CdTe is a very stable, non-toxic compound. Furthermore manufacturers take back these modules at the end of the life for controlled recycling.

CIS thin-film modules are normally fabricated onto a substrate, the back face, from the bottom up. The appearance is virtually black (**Fig. 2.10** and **Fig. 2.11**). Substrates can be glass, metal or plastic. Unlike amorphous silicon, CIS cells are not susceptible to light-induced degradation in performance.

Fig. 2.10 CIS thin-film modules on the roof of a detached house.
Photo courtesy: Würth Solar

Fig. 2.11 85 kW$_P$ CIS array at OpTIC in St Asaph (UK).
Photo courtesy: Avancis

Type	Typical module efficiency	Area requirement
high-performance hybrid silicon (HIT)	17–18%	6–7 m²/kW$_P$
monocrystalline silicon	12–15%	7–9 m²/kW$_P$
polycrystalline silicon	11–14%	7–10 m²/kW$_P$
thin-film CIS	9–11%	9–11 m²/kW$_P$
thin-film CdTe	6–8%	12–17 m²/kW$_P$
thin-film amorphous silicon	5–7%	14–20 m²/kW$_P$

2.2.5 High-performance PV cells

There are a wide range of new PV technologies being researched and developed in the pursuit of higher performance. One type to mention here, already well established in production, is the HIT PV cell, which stands for "heterojunction with intrinsic thin-layer".

HIT is a hybrid construction being a combination of a crystalline and thin-film silicon cell. Amorphous silicon is coated onto both front and rear faces of a monocrystalline silicon wafer. The interface is made by intrinsic (meaning undoped) silicon layers. Whereas a change in doping creates the necessary junction in a standard crystalline cell, here the junction is created between two structurally different semiconductors, hence the name heterojunction.

Compared to monocrystalline silicon, HIT cells are more efficient and have less degradation of efficiency with increase in operating temperature. This technology is used in case study 10.7.

In a bifacial PV cell, the back surface of the cell is processed in the same way as the front so as to absorb light. Bifacial PV cells are assembled into glass-glass laminates (see section 2.4) so that these modules allow effective use of the front and rear sides to generate at least 10% more electricity than the standard mono-facial type. This technology can be used in vertical installations, such as roadside sound barriers, where the sun illuminates both sides through the day. In a building application, the back side can benefit from ambient and reflected light so maximum gain is achieved with reflective or white objects behind. Bifacial transmit more infrared than monofacial cells so benefit from a lower operating temperature.

2.2.6 Comparison of PV technologies

The table above lists the established PV cell technologies in order of decreasing efficiency.

Also listed is the area requirement for the same power output (see 2.5 for the meaning of kW$_P$).

2.3 PV modules
2.3.1 Electrical connection

One PV cell produces only about 3 W at 0.6 V DC. For both a higher power unit and a higher voltage, 30 or more identical PV cells are connected in series to form a PV module, also known as a PV panel (Fig. 2.12). The PV module is the basic unit for building integration.

Under full illumination, a 36-cell module has an output voltage of about 17 V DC across its two output contacts. This DC current can be used to charge a battery (for off-grid applications) or converted to AC and at a higher voltage using a PV inverter. The module also performs the essential role of encapsulation (Fig. 2.13). This protects cells again mechanical stress, weathering and humidity. Only by lamination will they be able to operate for the required, and often guaranteed, 20–25 years or more, even in harsh environments.

2.3.2 Front glass

It is important that the covering glass has a very high transmission efficiency. White glass that is low in iron oxide is generally used. The glass is pre-stressed to enable it to withstand high thermal loading.

The basic transmission efficiency is about 92% and the remaining 8% reflection is reduced by about 3% by application of an anti-reflection coating to the front surface. (The back surface is not coated since it is in immediate contact with the encapsulation medium that has a similar refractive index.)

The standard glass is typically 3 or 4 mm thick, but increases to 10 mm for larger modules.

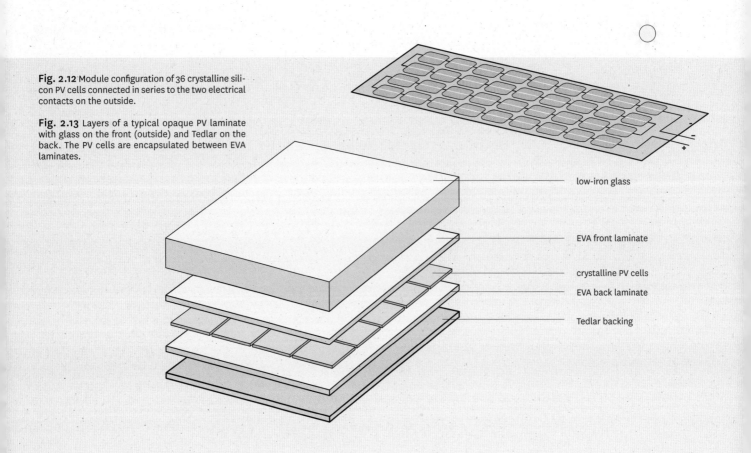

Fig. 2.12 Module configuration of 36 crystalline silicon PV cells connected in series to the two electrical contacts on the outside.

Fig. 2.13 Layers of a typical opaque PV laminate with glass on the front (outside) and Tedlar on the back. The PV cells are encapsulated between EVA laminates.

low-iron glass

EVA front laminate

crystalline PV cells

EVA back laminate

Tedlar backing

2.3.3 Encapsulation media and back face

The most common encapsulation is with cross-linkable ethylene vinyl acetate (EVA). The cells are laminated between films of EVA in a vacuum, under compression and up to 150°C. The EVA melts during this process and surrounds the cells on all sides. Note that EVA is not UV-resistant so depends on the front glass for UV screening. With very large modules, the cells can move around during the lamination process which makes it difficult to maintain equal gaps.

The backing in standard modules with EVA encapsulation is generally a thin opaque film, such as Tedlar (Dupont tradename for a film of polyvinyl fluoride, PVF), polyethylene terephthalate (PET) or metal **(Fig. 2.14, Fig. 2.15)**.
Alternatively the backing can be glass for transparency between the cells, and this type of module is known as a glass-glass laminate.

PV modules can also be integrated into double-glazed units. The PV panel would typically form the outer sheet of the double-glazed unit, to maximise the light penetration onto the PV cells. Single or double-glazed, the PV cells achieve high temperatures because of their dark appearance, so the glass laminate must be heat-treated (either heat-strengthened or fully tempered).
Polyvinyl butyral (PVB) has long been used in the glass industry as a sandwich layer in laminated safety glass (LSG), as required for instance in overhead glazing. PV glass-glass laminates with thin-film (amorphous) silicon or CIS with PVB encapsulation are available.

Another encapsulation medium is Teflon, the trade name for DuPont's amorphous fluoropolymer products, polytetrafluoroethylene (PTFE). In contrast to EVA, Teflon is UV resistant and has a lower reflectivity than glass. With these properties, Teflon can also provide the front protection dispensing with front glass. Instead the module can be laminated to a substrate, the back face, that can be a conventional tempered glass. The Teflon covering is only 0.5mm thick and thus conducts heat better than a thicker front glass would. This ensures good cooling where the back of the module might have poor ventilation. Teflon encapsulation is mostly used for small-scale modules, such as PV roof tiles.

In large glass-glass modules laminated with EVA, it is more difficult to reach the necessary 150°C for the best possible cohesion throughout the complete laminate. Resin encapsulation gets around this problem and can be applied to modules up to 2.5×3.8m. The PV cells need to be fixed between two glass sheets using adhesive pads to ensure their precise location. The sheets are bonded around the perimeter with a transparent spacer that completes the containment for the fluid resin. The resin is injected into the space and cured by UV light or other means.

Resin encapsulation can be used with sheets of Makrolon (the trade name used for the polycarbonate from Bayer MaterialScience) to form a glass-free module. Resin is also used for sound-absorbing glazing.

Fig. 2.14 Monocrystalline PV modules in a roof as an opaque panel with Tedlar on the back.
Photo courtesy: M.Art

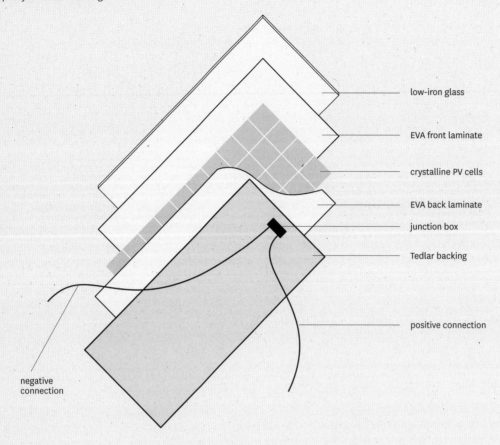

Fig. 2.15 Typical assembly, as seen from the back, of a crystalline silicon PV module made opaque by the Tedlar backing.

low-iron glass

EVA front laminate

crystalline PV cells

EVA back laminate

junction box

Tedlar backing

positive connection

negative connection

→ 2.3.3

Thermoplastic polyurethane (TPU) film has been developed for encapsulating PV cells, the same material as used to encapsulate car windscreens. TPU could also form the frame so there is the prospect of moulding a complete framed module in one step.

A new module concept being developed involves no encapsulation medium in direct contact with the PV cells but has the PV cells inside the cavity of a double-glazing unit. The cells are in an inert gas atmosphere and electrical interconnection is achieved by pressed contact. This has several advantages. There is no encapsulation material to age, a module can be repaired and the materials are easy to separate at end-of-life for recycling.

PV modules are exposed to weather like almost no other high-tech product, and still are expected to have extremely long life-spans. Manufacturers generally guarantee that their products will produce at least 80 percent of their nominal power after 20 to 25 years of operation, with total life-spans being somewhere beyond 30 years. Such a long life expectancy is achieved with durable packing and for this the encapsulation is crucial. Module producers are extremely conservative when it comes to innovations. After all, they take a considerable risk by offering such long guarantees so they tend to stay with technology proven as reliable in the past.

2.3.4 Thin-film encapsulation

In a thin-film module, although the series connection of thin-film cells for a module is a part the cell fabrication, this only produces a "raw module" that still requires encapsulation. Lamination with EVA film is the standard encapsulation method, as for crystalline modules. The back can be finished with Tedlar or a metal film.

Raw thin-film modules for amorphous silicon and CdTe are coated onto a superstrate which forms the front glass where light enters. It is not possible to use tempered glass for these superstrate sheets as the high temperature used for the semiconductor coating would destroy the glass strengthening. If the finished thin-film module is to fulfil demands for toughness, for instance in a façade, it must be laminated with a sheet of toughened safety glass. Amorphous silicon and CdTe are fabricated onto a superstrate, so any kind of glass can be used for the back.

CIS and amorphous silicon coated onto a substrate need a front glass. This needs to be low-iron "white" glass for high transparency.

Fig. 2.16 A range of standard PV modules in mono-crystalline silicon, polycrystalline silicon and thin film
Photo courtesy: M.Art

2.3.5 Cable outlets and junction boxes

From the cell strings embedded inside a module to the electrical contact points on the outside, either a rear glass panel with holes is used or the rear film is penetrated. In these cases, a junction box is fixed to the entry point. The module junction boxes must have minimum protection to IP 54 and Protection Class II.

Many modules are supplied complete with connecting leads and reverse polarity-proof, touch-proof plugs to make installation easy. The modules can then simply be plugged together without opening the module junction boxes.

Another possibility for the cable outlet is to turn the cables out along the glass edges. This option is used in custom-made modules where a junction box on the back would have a visually undesirable effect, such as in the vision panel of a façade.

2.3.6 Standard complete modules

Standard modules are designed to achieve the maximum energy yields at lowest cost. They are mostly glass-film laminates, with or without aluminium frames (Fig. 2.16). A frame improves the strength and rigidity of the module and helps mounting. Frameless modules are mounted into special profile systems.

Typical crystalline cells are square (often with chamfered corners) so they fit within the module with a minimum of gaps and thus of wasted space. Typical cell sizes are of length 100–150 mm. The cells are arranged in a variety of patterns to make a module. A typical standard module consists of 36 to 216 cells and has a peak power specification of 100 W_P to 300 W_P. The cells are arranged in 4 to 8 rows resulting in rectangular forms. Strings of 36 or 72 cells are connected in series. Larger modules use parallel connections of 2 or 3 of these strings.

These factors limit the available dimensions to several pre-established options.

2.3.7 Test standard

Standard modules are usually certified to international standards. These give assurance that the PV modules will perform under severe conditions.

For crystalline silicon modules, the relevant standard is IEC 61215 with the full title "Crystalline silicon terrestrial photovoltaic (PV) module—design qualification and type approval". IEC 61646 is the corresponding standard for thin-film modules.

For module certification, eight modules are selected at random from the production line. One module is used as a control, whilst the other seven modules are subject to various testing procedures to examine all parameters which are responsible for the ageing of PV modules. These include temperature variation from −40°C to 85°C, hail impact, high temperatures and relative humidity, local shadowing, static loading to 2400 Pa and wind loads up to 200 km/h.

The tests are judged to be passed, if after the qualification tests no major visual defects are detected and the output power has not or only slightly degraded from its initial value.

These two standards have become generally accepted as one of the quality marks for modules, particularly in Europe. It is demanded by most authorising authorities for national and international support programmes. However it is unusual for special and custom-made modules to be certified because of the high costs of the test for a low number of modules.

2.4 Module options
2.4.1 Bespoke size and shape

There is a limited range of standard module sizes since their dimensions are determined by the size of cell and number and layout of this cell size within the module. When designers are integrating modules into a façade, they will have to make a choice of either designing within the constraints of existing sizes or specifying a custom size.

The example integration shown in Chapter 3 in **Fig. 3.3** uses standard modules. The module width suits the space. For the vertical dimension, two modules are slightly taller than the floor-to-floor height but not enough to warrant a special module size. Another approach is to underfill a façade with standard modules and then fill the rest of the area to give the impression of complete coverage. The case study in section 8.5 uses this approach in which the corners of the façades had bespoke dummy modules with "dead cells". These use the same type of PV cells to ensure a uniform appearance but without any electrical connection. This case study also used plain painted steel panels at much lower cost in areas less critical in appearance.

When considering custom module sizes, the usual production schedules typical for the façade industry should be noted (see section 4.2.8 "Façade procurement").

If non-standard rectangular or non-rectangular modules are needed, it is important to note that all the cells in a series-connected string must be identical in size. Along the diagonal module edges of a non-rectangular module, there are two possibilities for cell coverage. The ends of the rows can be stepped back keeping within the diagonal edge, as in **Fig. 1.5**. This leaves uneven coverage but at least the cells are uncut and can be connected in series.

If complete coverage is needed for appearance, then cells can be cut parallel to it. The smaller size would reduce their current so they cannot be connected in series but must be left electrically inactive as "dead cells".

2.4.2 Cell arrangement and transparency

Semi-transparent and translucent PV modules present the designer with a wide range of possibilities to combine the production of electricity with natural lighting and create interesting light effects.

In a glass-glass laminate, some light passes through and this is referred to as semi-transparency or light-filtering (**Fig. 2.17**, **Fig. 2.18**). Given that crystalline cells are opaque, the amount of light passing through is simply determined by the spacing between cells. The space between individual cells can be adjusted from 1 to about 30 mm (**Fig. 2.14** and **Fig. 2.17**). Cells are individually connected to each other but the electric wiring is not visible unless viewed close up. The area of modules needed for the required power output when using semi-transparent modules will increase roughly in proportion to the proportion of the modules that is transparent.

A finer form of semi-transparency can be achieved with crystalline cells by covering them with small perforations. One process machines grooves onto both sides of the cells. The direction of the grooves in the front and back are rotated by 90° to each other. At the points where the grooves cross, they break through creating smooth holes. In another method, small perforations are cut by laser.

Thin-film modules have other options for semi-transparency. The cell spacing can be increased for strip-like transparency. Alternatively the lines of material can be removed perpendicular to the cell strips. Combined with spaced cells, this creates a fine checked pattern that gives an even neutrally coloured average transparency and transmission values of 10–15%.

There are some technological developments in which the thin-film is truly translucent but these are not in commercial production. In most cases where translucent is mentioned, this is just referring to semi-transparent, as described here.

Fig. 2.17 Monocrystalline PV in a semitransparent module (glass on the back). Photo courtesy: M.Art

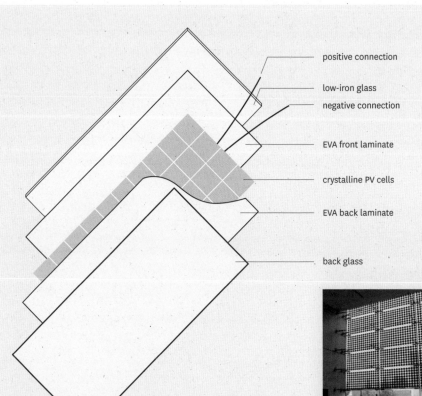

positive connection

low-iron glass

negative connection

EVA front laminate

crystalline PV cells

EVA back laminate

back glass

Fig. 2.18 Typical assembly, seen from the back, of a crystalline silicon module that is semi-transparent by having a back glass. Electrical connections are formed in the edge of the laminate.

Fig. 2.19 A large area of semitransparent PV modules formed by opaque crystalline cells laminated with glass on both sides. Photo courtesy: M.Art

Fig. 2.20 A mixture of clear vision panels and semi-transparent PV modules. Photo courtesy: M.Art

2.4.3 Colour and texture

PV cells usually have a dark appearance because they are designed to reflect a minimum of light, in order to produce maximum electricity output. Monocrystalline silicon PV cells are typically black, grey or blue, while polycrystalline silicon cells are usually medium or dark blue. The appearance of thin-film amorphous silicon cells is uniform, with a dark mat surface; colours include grey, brown and black. Cells based on CIS and CdTe are dark brown to black.

By varying the thickness of the anti-reflection coating, other colours can be obtained, such as the multi-coloured polycrystalline cells shown here (Fig. 2.21). But by doing this, the overall reflection will increase and the efficiency will decrease by 15–30% depending on the colour. These modules are considered as custom-made products, and their price can be two or three times the price of normal cells.

The glass laminate that supports the PV cells can be modified to provide a different appearance of the panel, by using the available glass techniques.

A ceramic silk-screen frit can be applied to the back pane of a glass laminate PV module to achieve the required aesthetics. In the case study in section 6.6, one of the glass laminates has been treated to provide a translucent diffusive appearance.

A large range of patterns and colours of ceramic fritting is available. Ceramic fritting is often used to produce look-alike glass units, to be installed where PV modules would be inappropriate, such as permanently shaded areas.

A printed or coloured interlayer can be built into a glass laminate PV module, below the silicon cell. Interlayers may have printed photographic images applied.

Fig. 2.21 Examples of the coloured effects on polycrystalline silicon cells created by varying the thickness of the anti-reflection coating.
Photo courtesy: Sunways AG

2.4.4 Flexible and curved modules

Flexible PV cells are a relatively new product that allows attractive building integrated options.

Curved modules with a minimum radius of 0.9 m can be fabricated from crystalline PV cells by embedding the cells between curved sheets or curving finished modules. Thin-film modules are permanently flexible and rollable when deposited onto malleable substrates.

Flexible and curved modules are not laminated in hard glass but on a versatile material, e.g. metal and synthetic foils, synthetic resin and glass textile membranes. This is also made possible by new thin layer technologies. The flexible PV modules can be quite light and have been used for arched construction elements, as awnings, flexible roofing with integrated PV cells.

When thin-film amorphous silicon is deposited onto a substrate, the reverse of that in **Fig. 2.9**, then metal or plastic sheeting can be used which are flexible. Such a system can be rolled onto a standing seam metal roof (**Fig. 2.22**).

Crystalline cells can be laminated with acrylic plastic or Makrolon. The minimal cold-bending radius for cell arrays of 10 × 10 cm is 350 times the thickness of the strongest acrylic plastic sheet.

Very few curved glass applications exist incorporating PV cells. Wafer-type cells cannot be easily bent as they fracture in a brittle manner. Often acrylic/ polycarbonate plexi-glass is used to avoid the issues associated with glass bending. Curved glass laminates incorporating wafer-type cells would be a bespoke and very costly solution.

Thin-film cells are created by a deposition process, which requires a substrate with a flat surface. Therefore, thin-film cells cannot be applied to bent glass. Applying the film first and then bending the glass is also not possible because the cells would get damaged during the glass bending process.

Flexible and curved PV cells can however be created by laminating thin-film PV cells in to flexible substrates such as synthetic foils, synthetic resins, textile, membranes, sheet metals, etc. The flexible PV modules can be light-weight and used for arched construction elements, flexible roofing, etc (**Fig. 2.22**).

It should be noted that curved modules will have a reduced performance due to the non-uniformity of the sunlight intensity over the module surface.

Fig. 2.22 Roll of flexible roofing PV using thin-film amorphous silicon.
Photo courtesy: M.Art

2.5 PV module specification and standard test conditions

The most common way to compare modules is by their peak-power specification given as watts peak or W_P, sometimes known as the "boiler-plate" specification. This rating is made at a well-defined set of conditions known as standard test conditions (STC):
— the actual temperature of the PV cells (25°C or 77°F),
— the intensity of radiation (1 kW/m^2),
— the spectral distribution of the light (air mass 1.5 or AM 1.5, the spectrum of sunlight that has been filtered by passing through 1.5 thicknesses of the earth's atmosphere).

These conditions correspond to noon on a clear sunny day with the sun about 60 degrees above the horizon, the PV module directly facing the sun, and an air temperature of 0°C (32°F).

In reality these conditions occur very rarely. When the sun shines with the specified intensity, the cell temperature would be higher than 25°C. For this reason, the nominal operating cell temperature (NOCT) is often specified as well. This cell temperature is determined for an irradiance level of 800 W/m^2, an ambient temperature of 20°C and a wind velocity of 1 m/s.

In production, PV modules are tested in a chamber known as a flash simulator. This device contains a flash bulb and filter designed to mimic sunlight as closely as possible. Because the flash takes place in only 50 milliseconds, the cells do not heat up appreciably. This allows the electrical characteristics of the module to be measured at a single temperature, the ambient temperature of the module/factory, usually close to 25°C.

Note:
— Peak power in W_P is merely a convenient way to compare the performance of modules. In no way can it be related to the output power of a conventional generator or the peak electrical demand of a building, say. (See "specific yield" in Chapter 3.)
— Cell temperatures in operation are usually well above 25°C, causing a drop in peak power. (See "Effect of temperature" in Chapter 3.)

3. PV FOR DESIGNERS

3.1 Location constraints

Here are two examples that exemplify the extremes of challenges for BIPV placement on a building. The Solar Office, Doxford International Business Park, a 73 kW$_P$ BIPV façade (**Fig. 3.3**), is highly optimised for solar collection: facing south, next to a car park, so free from any shading, and with a façade tilted 30° back from vertical for a better angle to the noon sun.

In contrast, 10 Whitfield Street (**Fig. 3.1**) is an infill development in a dense urban context. The architect had to work within tight spatial constraints. Since the top of the building already had solar water heating and a brown roof, opportunity for BIPV was left as the southern face of a bay window. An array of six PV modules were be fitted forming a 1.6 kW$_P$ array, to generate power while at the same time reducing solar gain to the internal space (**Fig. 3.2**). Though a small array in a less-than-optimal position, it does contribute to wider appreciation of renewable energy and general awareness simply by its street-level presence.

This chapter looks at the site and building type, both being key factors in assessing the suitability of a building for PV and specifically BIPV. Where there is flexibility in the design of a new building, PVs should be fully considered at the outset since the PV array can influence the building's orientation, footprint, layout and form. However where form is dictated by other factors, opportunities for PV on a building need to be examined systematically, as follows:

— 3.2 Tilt and orientation of building surfaces available
— 3.3 Assessing the degree of overshadowing
— 3.4 Grouping of modules for electrical connection
— 3.5 Minimising partial shading
— 3.6 Temperature effect and ventilation
— 3.7 Potential power output

Fig. 3.1 A typical central London location with buildings crowded together. This view is looking south onto the bay window of 10 Whitfield Street on the left.
Photo: Simon Roberts

Fig. 3.2 The south-facing side of the bay window has a 1.6 kW$_P$ array. The PV modules are clearly visible at street level to passers-by.
Photo: Simon Roberts

Fig. 3.3 Looking north across the car park to the 73 kW$_P$ BIPV façade of the Solar Office, Doxford International (UK).
Photo courtesy: Schüco International KG

3.2 Effect of tilt and orientation

3.2.1 Solar principles

As part of the design process, the tilt and orientation of the façades that will incorporate PV elements is a starting point. In order to understand the significance of tilt and orientation, we need to appreciate how light reaches building surfaces. Irradiance is the amount of light incident on a surface at one point in time. Global irradiance onto a site is a combination of direct and diffuse irradiance. Direct irradiance is dependent on the sun's position and the sun's path tracing a range of angles through the day and year (Fig. 3.4). Diffuse irradiance arrives at a surface from clouds and haze, and also makes a contribution to PV output.

Insolation, a shortened form of incoming solar radiation, is the total amount of light energy received at a particular angle over a period of time, such as a whole year. For the northern hemisphere, a permanently open southerly aspect is the obvious requirement. The maximum annual PV output corresponds to a south orientation and a tilt from the horizontal equal to the latitude of the site minus about 20°. This angle comes from the fact that peak insolation takes place in summer, when the sun is higher than the latitude of the site. By orienting the panels preferably to the summer irradiation, the annual output will then be higher.

Fig. 3.4 Range of sun paths over the year for the summer solstice and winter solstice. The angle of these paths would be for Europe or a similar northern latitude.

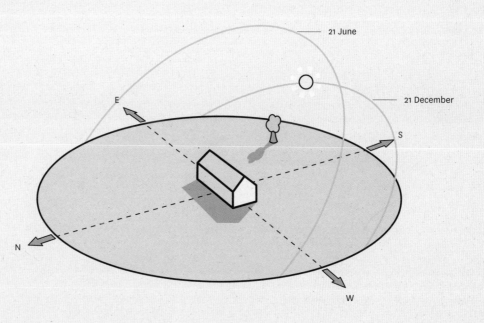

3.2.2 Non-optimal tilt and orientation

Unlike a ground- or roof-mounted PV system, a BIPV installation may have to consider non-optimal orientations. To compare options for a given project, we can use design tools such as global insolation charts for the area of our site. **Fig. 3.5** shows one of those charts which is for Freiburg, Germany. For all possible tilts and orientations that a PV module can be mounted, these charts combine the direct and diffuse irradiance for typical annual weather at a given location. They map the decrease in insolation compared to the direction for the maximum.

For easier interpretation, we can pick values from the global insolation chart of **Fig. 3.5** to put on the facets of a building as in **Fig. 3.6**. In this example, the total annual output is over 90% of maximum for the three 45° roof facets facing southward. The roof sides and top are above 75% of maximum while the sides of the building are above 55% of maximum. This shows that the vertical angle has an important effect on performance whereas less critical is the orientation anywhere between southeast and southwest.

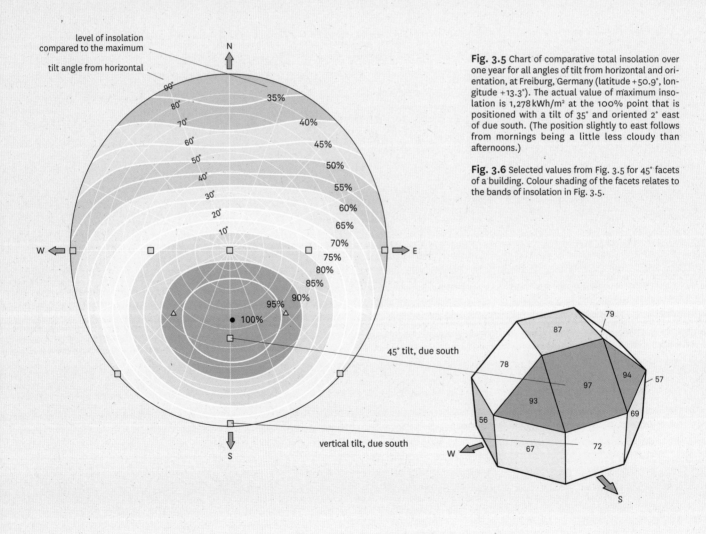

Fig. 3.5 Chart of comparative total insolation over one year for all angles of tilt from horizontal and orientation, at Freiburg, Germany (latitude +50.9°, longitude +13.3°). The actual value of maximum insolation is 1,278 kWh/m² at the 100% point that is positioned with a tilt of 35° and oriented 2° east of due south. (The position slightly to east follows from mornings being a little less cloudy than afternoons.)

Fig. 3.6 Selected values from Fig. 3.5 for 45° facets of a building. Colour shading of the facets relates to the bands of insolation in Fig. 3.5.

Fig. 3.7 Sun-path analysis for a building on a February day at 10 am. Four zones of equal area have been added to illustrate issues relating to orientation, tilt and overshadowing.

Fig. 3.8 Sun-path analysis for a building at 12 pm with the same zones as in Fig. 3.7.

Fig. 3.9 Sun-path analysis for a building at 2 pm with the same zones as in Fig. 3.7.

3.3 Overshadowing and BIPV options
3.3.1 Examining overshadowing

The efficiency of PV systems is influenced by many factors, but the most important of all is the overshadowing.
It is recommended that the process of examining a particular building for its BIPV potential starts with a 3D model and a sun-path analysis.

The example in **Figs. 3.7, 3.8** and **3.9** is of a building in London for one day in February at 10 am, 12 pm and 2 pm, respectively. The example shows a simple block structure above the two stories of the main body of the building. The long axis of this block is aligned north-west to south-east and the block casts a shadow across the roof from morning to afternoon.

Let us suppose that there are four zones of equal area being considered for possible BIPV installation. These are shown by the numbered rectangles in the figures.
Zones 1, 2 and 3 are all free from overshadowing so would make good locations for PV. Note that area 2 is at a different tilt to zones 1 and 3. The previous section shows that it will generate a different amount of power. Furthermore the difference in instantaneous irradiance will have an influence on how the parts of the PV installation are connected electrically. This aspect is discussed in the next section.

Area 4 is affected by overshadowing so is not ideal for PV. However it is totally free of overshadowing in the afternoon. Also the sun is higher in the sky later in the year so overshadowing in the morning will be less than as shown in **Fig. 3.7**. To estimate the reduction in electrical output, proprietary software, such as PV-SYST, should be used. Since there is occasional overshadowing of area 4, this has an influence on electrical connections, as covered in the next section.

This example has been about overshadowing by part of a building on itself. Shading resulting from the location covers all shading produced from the building's surroundings. Neighbouring buildings, trees and even distant tall buildings can shade a system, or at least lead to horizon darkening. It must be taken into account that, due to the growth of trees and shrubs, vegetation may shade the system only after a couple of years.

So the 3D model should be extended to include neighbouring buildings to check for all possibilities of overshadowing. The analysis should be carried out for three days of year: usually winter solstice (21st December), spring equinox (21st March) and summer solstice (21st June). Each day should then be examined at hourly steps through the day identifying where the overshadowing will occur.

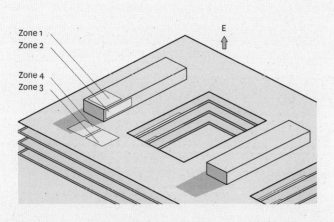

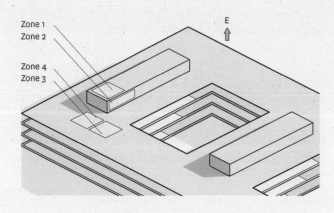

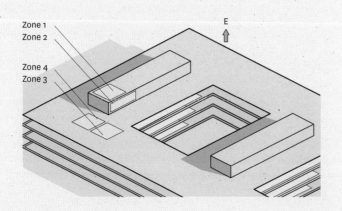

3.3.2 Principles for minimising overshadowing

Within a development of many building, there will be a tendency for them to over-shadow each other. Where possible, PV installations should be located at the northern side of a space that is likely to remain permanently open. If planning on the scale of a city block, taller buildings should be placed on the northern side and stepped down progressively to lower buildings on the southern side.

With a new building development, additional factors to consider include whether there will be later planting and other new buildings in the immediate vicinity. In addition, the extent of tree growth should also be taken into account.

California even has a Solar Shade Control Act of 1979. It relates to trees or shrubs on one property shading a solar collector on a neighbouring property. Specifically, the shadow cast should be no greater than 10% of the collector absorption area of the solar collector surface at any one time between the hours of 10 am and 2 pm.

To sum up, a building orientated to the south (in the northern hemisphere) for day-lighting, passive solar gain and free of overshading is eminently suitable for PVs. Similarly, a footprint with the long axis running east-west thus giving a large south-facing wall area and potentially a large south-facing roof is advantageous for PVs. Self-shading by the structure's own architectural form should be avoided or minimised. The main strategies to prevent self-shading at the design stage are as follows:

— For roof arrays, put potential obstacles to north, such as lift rooms, water tanks, chimneys and ventilation stacks (Fig. 3.10).
— For façade arrays, put staircases to the north (Fig. 3.11).
— Separate trees from PV façades and if possible use deciduous trees which are free of leaves in winter when shadows are long.

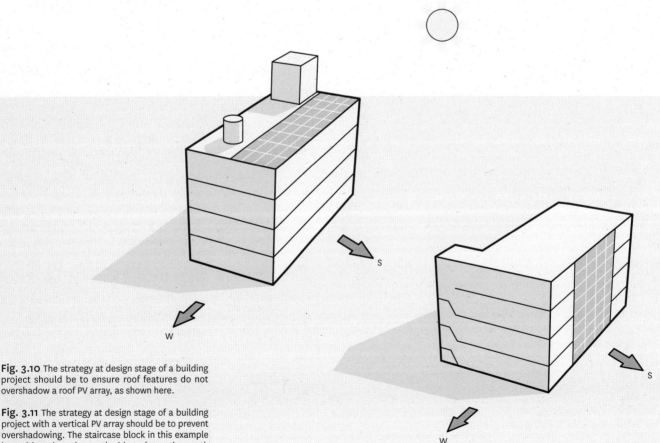

Fig. 3.10 The strategy at design stage of a building project should be to ensure roof features do not overshadow a roof PV array, as shown here.

Fig. 3.11 The strategy at design stage of a building project with a vertical PV array should be to prevent overshadowing. The staircase block in this example is positioned on the north side to leave the south side clear.

3.4 Connection concepts
3.4.1 Inverters

With no or low shading and PV modules all at the same angle, the possible yields will be independent of the PV array configuration. The designer can leave the details of configuration wiring to the electrical specialist.

However where parts of the PV installation receive different levels of irradiance, it is very helpful to have a basic understanding of some connection principles since this can have an impact on design.

The PV module is the basic unit as far as the installation is concerned. A module's output is DC at around 30V (depending on the number of PV cells connected in series). The electrical interface from this DC to the higher voltage AC of the network is an inverter. In most installations, several modules are connected to share the same inverter.

Inverters are available as central inverters for an entire system, as string inverters for a string of modules and as module inverters for an individual module. Each of the three concepts has advantages and disadvantages. Which concept is chosen depends upon the type of application. The approach of two or more string inverters should be considered for systems consisting of sub-array zones with different orientations and tilts, or for systems that are partially shaded, as described here.

3.4.2 String inverters

Where possible, PV modules are connected in series to form a "string" in order for their voltages to add (Fig. 3.12). Connecting modules in series strings is desirable for two reasons:
— the wiring size is kept small,
— inverters are more efficient and cost-effective at higher voltage.

Exactly the same electric current passes through each module in the series. Since the current doesn't increase, the wiring size (cross-section of copper conductor) can remain constant. With the alternative arrangement of connecting modules in parallel, they all share the same low voltage but their final output at the inverter has a high current necessitating thick conductors (Fig. 3.13).

Given production tolerances, modules are best sorted by current to reduce mismatch losses in a series string. Solar array inverters perform another important role. They adjust to the particular output characteristic of PV modules using a "maximum power point tracker" (MPPT). As the irradiance varies from moment to moment, the MPPT part adjusts the precise DC operating voltage the PV array is working at. The voltage is automatically adjusted in order that the product of current and voltage (value of current multiplied by the value of voltage) is as high as possible, this being the maximum power.

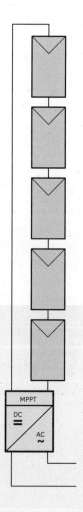

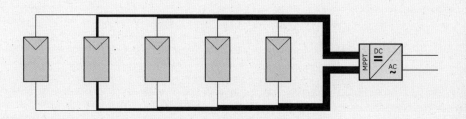

Fig. 3.12 Series connection of PV modules to an inverter. Note how the same current passes through all modules so the connection wiring does not need to increase in thickness for each module added. (MPPT: maximum power point tracker)

Fig. 3.13 Parallel connection of PV modules to an inverter. The diagram shows schematically how the conductor needs to increase in thickness as each module contributes current. (MPPT: maximum power point tracker)

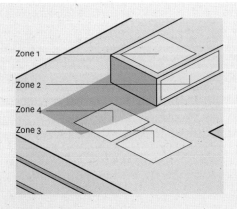

Zone 1
Zone 2
Zone 4
Zone 3

→ 3.4.2

Fig. 3.14 is a close-up of **Fig. 3.7** showing the four zones. Zones 1 and 2 are at different tilts. Therefore they will always be subject to different irradiance conditions. If modules in the two zones were connected in one series string, the resulting current would be determined by the minimum, this being from the modules receiving least irradiance. Such an arrangement would hold back the full generating potential of the modules that are receiving a higher irradiance.

The four zones could be connected as separate series strings, as in **Fig. 3.15**. Each zone is effectively separate on the DC side and each string MPPT can optimise voltage and current according to the irradiance and if partially shaded. The outputs of the strings only come together at the common AC voltage, whether they are generating a high or low current.

3.4.3 Zoning a PV array

Owing to simpler and more cost-effective mounting, string inverters can provide the better solution economically. From this approach follows some general principles when zoning a PV array, as in **Fig. 3.14**:

— Keep zones sufficiently large for a high voltage.
— Where possible, design for zones of equal area (thus made up of equal numbers of PV modules) so that there is only one size of inverter in use, which helps with maintenance and replacement.
— All modules within a zone to receive the same irradiance (to be at the same tilt and orientation).
— Where there are two or more zones on one facet of a building, plan for the zones to follow the pattern of overshadowing, so keeping shaded modules together.

Zoning a PV array into equal areas adds a constraint. Some zones may underfill the facet available. To maintain a uniform appearance, non-functioning dummy PV-modules or look-alike panels may be needed. Both solutions have been used in case study 6.5 of The Co-operative Insurance Tower.

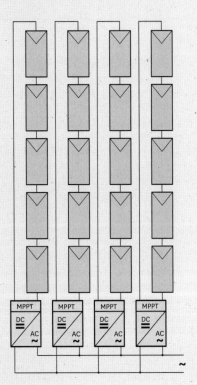

Fig. 3.14 Close-up of the building in Fig. 3.7 showing the four zones.

Fig. 3.15 An array of 20 PV modules connected in strings to four separate inverters. (MPPT: maximum power point tracker)

Fig. 3.16 Example of PV modules clear of any shading by details of the façade.
Photo courtesy: Schüco International KG

Fig. 3.17 Schematic to emphasise that shading of just one cell of a PV module reduces the electricity output markedly, just as water is prevented from flowing in a hose when one part is squeezed.

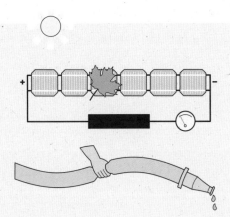

3.5 Partial shading

Solar cells work best if they are illuminated uniformly. Clearly overshadowing, described earlier in this chapter, is going to reduce output. However even partial shading from an adjacent chimney, tree branch or lamp post which might appear quite minor can reduce the electricity output significantly. Overhead cables running over the building that cast a small shadow even have a negative effect.

The effect of partial shading can be understood in analogy with liquid flowing in a hose (**Fig. 3.17**). The charge carriers which enable PV material to conduct electricity are only present in PV material when it is illuminated. So shading one cell not only stops it generating power but stops current generation, so the cell becomes an electrical resistor.

When one cell is covered, current from the other illuminated cells is driven through the darkened cell. This could cause a problem but bypass diodes are fitted in modules as normal practice to avoid overheating. A bypass diode is usually connected across eighteen to twenty cells. Two bypass diodes would be fitted to a 36-cell module. If one cell in such a module were covered, the output voltage would be halved through the protective effect of the bypass diode, but the output power would also be halved.

For a thin object such as a cable or handrail, the closer the object the darker the shadow. By increasing the separation, the shadow losses definition as it becomes larger. This has less effect on electrical output since the shading is not concentrated on a few cells. Care needs to be taken with details near a module. **Fig. 3.16** is an example of avoiding any features proud of the PV modules.

3.6 Temperature effect and ventilation
3.6.1 Effect of heat

In a solar water heater for instance, the higher the temperature, the better the performance. PV technologies are quite different because their efficiency decreases when module temperature increases.

PV modules convert 10–15% of the solar energy into electricity. Therefore the vast majority of the incident energy is converted into heat. For crystalline silicon cells, the efficiency changes almost linearly by –0.4% for every degree rise in temperature. For amorphous silicon cells, the effect is roughly half this depending on the specific production process. The temperature difference between PV and ambient depends on irradiation intensity and can climb by more than 40°C. In the summer, with high ambient temperatures, the PV temperature can therefore reach about 70° to 75°C.

Module manufacturers sometimes specify the nominal operating cell temperature (NOCT). This cell temperature is determined for an irradiance of $800 \, W/m^2$, an ambient temperature of 20°C and a wind velocity of 1 m/s.

3.6.2 Power reduction values

The temperature the PV actually reaches depends on how well it can dissipate the heat. If the PV is insulated at the rear side, it can only lose heat at the front side, which reduces its heat loss capability. If possible, an air gap should be created between the PV and the building structure behind, which allows cooling of the PV laminate by natural convection **(Fig. 3.18)**.

Here are some indicative values of power reduction for crystalline silicon modules in various roof mountings, as compared to the power output of a completely free-standing array which would be just 22°C warmer than ambient:
— with a large gap –1.8% (28°C warmer)
— with good ventilation –2.1% (29°C warmer)
— with poor ventilation –2.6% (32°C warmer)
— with no ventilation –5.4% (43°C warmer)

A vertical façade is less well cooled than a roof installation. Here are indicative values of power reduction for a vertical façade, again compared to a free-standing array:
— with good ventilation –3.9% (35°C warmer)
— with poor ventilation –4.8% (39°C warmer)
— with no ventilation –8.9% (55°C warmer)

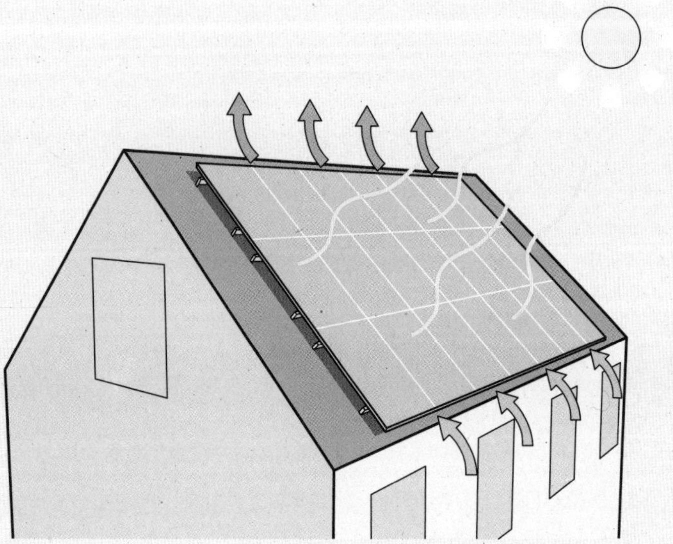

Fig. 3.18 Where possible it is recommended that the PV modules dissipate the heat gain from solar irradiation. This schematic shows installation of an array on a roof where a gap between the PV and the building envelope encourages natural convection to assist cooling.

3.7 Location and performance

Once a building has been assessed for PV feasibility, the potential performance of electrical output can be estimated.

3.7.1 Daily insolation

The starting point for an estimate of electrical output is clearly the amount of solar energy received at the location. A useful quantity is the average daily insolation, often in energy units of kWh (not to be confused with electrical energy, which uses the same unit).

Daily insolation varies through the year, increasing with day length and altitude of the sun. **Fig. 3.19** shows the daily insolation as monthly average values for a northern latitude site. Insolation also takes into account the weather and cloud pattern of the area. In this example the weather accounts for the lower level in October compared to the equivalent time in March which has the same day lengths.

For grid-connected PV systems, energy production is normally considered over the whole year. Therefore daily insolation can be averaged over all seasons for an annual average value. These figures are mapped as a set of curves for all parts of the world, as in **Fig. 3.20**. This data is taken from many years of climatic data so represents a "typical" year.

The insolation over a whole year span will be maximum when the surface has a tilt about 20° less than the latitude angle, and where north of the Tropic of Cancer (in the northern hemisphere) is oriented south. Note that the map of values in **Fig. 3.20** is for a horizontal surface, called the average daily global horizontal solar radiation. Other types of maps show values for a flat surface tilted south (for the northern latitudes) at an angle equal to the latitude. The tilt increases the values for higher latitude sites compared to those shown in the map.

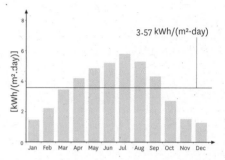

Fig. 3.19 Example of monthly averages of daily insolation at a northern latitude site. The highest monthly value (in July) is almost 6 kWh/(m²·day) and lowest (in December) is 1.3 kWh/(m²·day). The annual average is 3.57 kWh/(m²·day).

Fig. 3.20 Annual average of daily insolation on a horizontal plane (tilt = 0°) across the world. The conversion from values on the map of kWh/(m²·day) to some equivalent units is below:

kWh/(m²·day)	kWh/(m²·y)	MJ/(m²·y)
1	365	1.3
2	730	2.6
3	1095	3.9
4	1460	5.3
5	1825	6.6
6	2190	7.9
7	2555	9.2

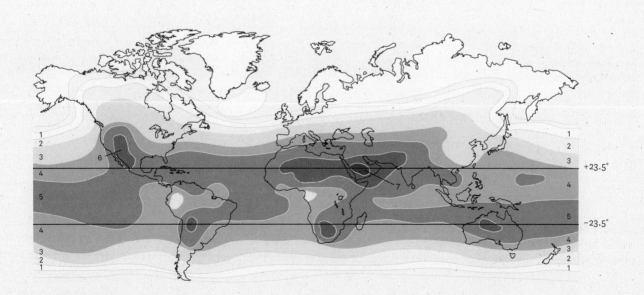

3.7.2 Electrical output

We can now bring together the main factors that determine the total electrical output from a PV installation over a year:
— Annual average daily insolation (section 3.7.1)
— Tilt and orientation of PV array (see **Fig. 3.6**).
— Whether there will be any overshadowing or partial shading (see **Fig. 3.17**).
— Extent of solar heating (or ineffectiveness of ventilation cooling, **Fig. 3.18**).
— Efficiency of the balance-of-system components (section 2.1).
— Efficiency of PV module, as dependent on the type of PV material (section 2.5).

There are many PV software packages available to carry out this calculation.
Just to give an idea of what the calculation might look like, here are some example values:
— Data available for the site for average daily insolation might be $3.5\,kWh/(m^2{\cdot}day)$ for a horizontal surface and $4.0\,kWh/(m^2{\cdot}day)$ at the optimum tilt that maximises output.
— A vertical surface facing south might have a relative efficiency of 72% compared to the optimum tilt.
— The south face might be free of shading.
— Heating of the PV system may reduce the output by 4%.
— Balance of system losses might be 15%.

The estimate of annual output per kW_P of the PV system would be:
annual output = 365 days/y $\cdot\,4.0\,kWh/(m^2{\cdot}day)\cdot 72\%\cdot 96\%\cdot 85\%$
= $860\,kWh$ (electrical)/y

If the PV array is monocrystalline silicon with $8\,m^2/kW_P$ (section 2.5), then an area of $8\,m^2$ is estimated to generate $860\,kWh/y$ of electricity, or $1\,m^2$ would generate about $175\,kWh/y$.

3.7.3 Specific yield

A useful parameter making use of generation data from existing nearby PV installations is the specific yield. This is the energy generated divided by the "boilerplate" or STC rating given as $kWh/(kW_P{\cdot}y)$. In other words, "how much energy (kWh) is produced over one year by a specific quantity of installed PV modules ($1\,kW_P$)".
The energy part is a figure read directly from an electricity meter, thus taking into account reduction in system output caused by losses associated with balance-of-system (BOS) components such as inverters, resistance of wiring and load matching. There are many factors wrapped up in this figure including latitude, weather, orientation, type of installation as well as how well the system was designed and maintained. Therefore a comparison should be made for similar installations in similar conditions.
For the case studies featured in this handbook, their performance is collated in Chapter 13 including their specific yields. Example values:
— System in Hamburg, Germany, on a vertical surface facing south: $599\,kWh/(kW_P{\cdot}y)$
— System in San Francisco, USA, on a horizontal surface: $1238\,kWh/(kW_P{\cdot}y)$

4. DESIGN OF THE BUILDING ENVELOPE

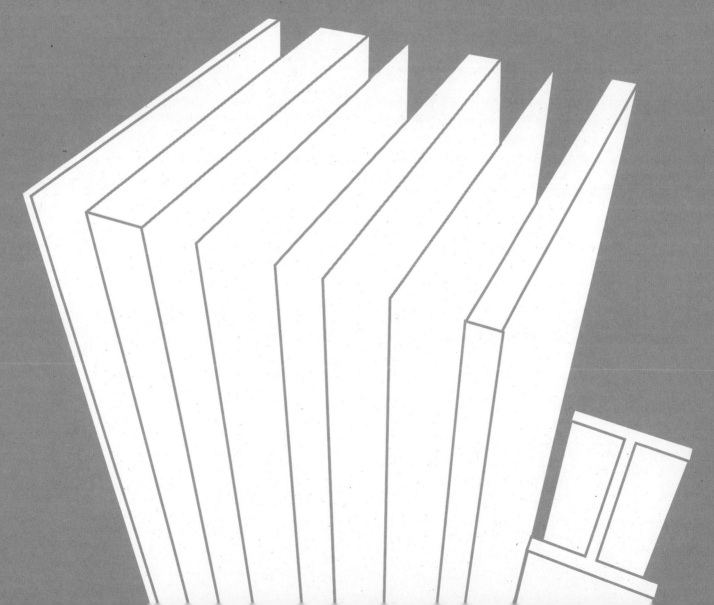

4.1 Building envelope integration

Lay-on PV modules are designed for one purpose only: the generation of electricity using solar power. This handbook concerns building integration where the PV elements also have to play the same role as the traditional wall-, window- or roofing-cladding elements they replace.

The building envelope represents the interface between the controlled internal environment and the variable external climate. It needs to achieve a certain level of airtightness to avoid unnecessary space heating and cooling due to infiltration (uncontrolled ventilation) and to enable effective performance of ventilation systems. It needs to be weathertight and for this aim the cladding design should incorporate multiple lines of defence against water ingress. Finally a façade needs to mediate the transfer of heat between the internal and external environment in order to create a comfortable indoor environment while using the minimum amount of energy.

Beyond the thermally protective function, building-envelopes are designed to withstand wind loads and imposed loads such as barrier loading, impact loading and loading due to cleaning and maintenance. Bomb blast loading and seismic affects may also need to be considered.

The façade presents also a regulation and control function for daylight, ventilation, solar heat gains and privacy and a safety and containment function.

A new list of requirements must be addressed by a building-integrated PV system:
— Colour, image, size
— Weather-tightness
— Wind loading
— Durability and maintenance
— Safety during construction and in use (fire, electrical, stability)
— Cost

The appropriateness of the integration is influenced by the design, the materials and the surface finishes, also the size, proportion and subdivision of the components. These must always take into account the constructional system as a whole. In order to fulfil both requirements—those from construction and those from energy production (Chapter 3)—it is critical that PV integration is discussed from the beginning of the design process.

4.2 PV integration opportunities

This chapter gives an overview of the different façade systems where photovoltaic panels can be applied. **Fig. 4.1** shows a classification of the different façades, as later described in detail in each chapter of Part 2 of this handbook:

— Shading (Chapter 5) is the simplest type of integration since it is essentially an add-on structure, but still fulfilling a dual function of protection from excessive solar gain as well as generation of power.

— A rainscreen (Chapter 6) applies to traditional building construction where PV is the outer leaf.

— Stick system (Chapter 7) is a type of lightweight curtain wall but constructed on-site so necessitating scaffold. PV modules can replace the opaque or vision panels.

— Unitised (Chapter 8) is another type of curtain wall but with factory-made units which can be installed on-site without scaffold. It is the method of preference for high-rise buildings.

— Double-skin façade (Chapter 9) is a high-performance design that takes a variety of forms.

— Atria and canopies (Chapter 10) are horizontal or sloping surfaces where PV modules can be used.

— Glazing systems are covered in Chapters 7 and 8.

Fig. 4.1 PV-integration options, as covered in Part 2 of this handbook.

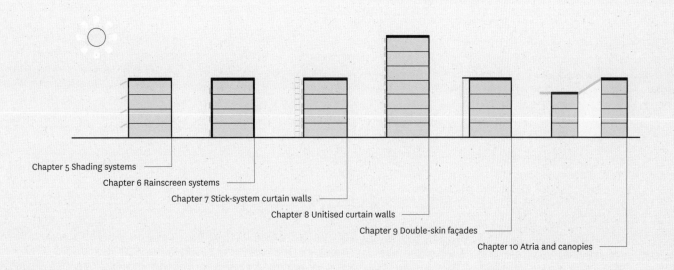

Chapter 5 Shading systems

Chapter 6 Rainscreen systems

Chapter 7 Stick-system curtain walls

Chapter 8 Unitised curtain walls

Chapter 9 Double-skin façades

Chapter 10 Atria and canopies

4.2.1 Sunshades and sunscreens

The architectural drive to improve the comfort of building occupants with respect to daylighting and views to the outside has led to the desire for large vision areas. These often require shading devices, such as louvres, to limit excessive solar gains. External louvres, both horizontal and vertical, fixed or adjustable, metal or glazed, can be mounted close or at a distance to the envelope. They are fixed back with bracketry, either simply to the cladding frame or directly to the building structure through penetration in the cladding.
The main issues related to external louvres are their resistance to wind loading, durability and access for cleaning and maintenance.
Sunshades are good surfaces for PV modules because of the tilt and ventilation (Fig. 4.2). The main issue is the self-shadowing of louvres onto each other under some sun angles which reduces output-power performance.
Sunscreens are sunshades closer to vertical and moderating transmission. If tilted to the adequate inclination and properly oriented, they can provide protection from direct sunlight and a high PV output.

4.2.2 Rainscreen cladding

From a structural point of view, we can distinguish between two fundamental types of façade:
— load-bearing external wall
— non load-bearing facing leaf

Rainscreens described in this section are used with the first, while the second, known as curtain walling, is described later.

Traditionally in Europe and countries with similar climatic conditions, external walls were built of load-bearing masonry, first using stone and, later, brick (Fig. 4.3). Mortar is used to hold together and seal the blocks. To protect the mortar joints against rain, render is often applied. Windows are installed or integrated within the load-bearing exterior walls, either as single "punched" windows or combined to form continuous bands of windows. Besides traditional masonry, these days load-bearing walls are also manufactured from concrete.

Particularly in damp climates, moisture damage on sides exposed to heavy rain eventually led to the introduction of cavity-wall masonry. The penetration of moisture from outside towards the inside is interrupted by an air gap between the outer and inner skin. At the same time, ventilation of the cavity facilitates drying out. With a cavity wall, it is also no longer necessary to have external render.

Fig. 4.2 PV modules integrated in shading devices of an office building in London (UK).
Photo: Keith Morrison
Courtesy: Romag

Fig. 4.3 An example of load-bearing masonry wall as used traditionally in Europe and countries with similar climatic conditions.
Photo courtesy: Arup

Fig. 4.4 An example of rainscreen cladding with terracotta.
Photo courtesy: Arup

Fig. 4.5 An example of a rainscreen with partial cladding in metal.
Photo: Graham Gaunt
Courtesy: Arup

The same effect of a moisture barrier can be achieved with different types of cladding as the external leaf or rainscreen. Slate, tiles and timber cladding were used originally. Later, stone or plastic panels, fibre boards, metal sheeting or coloured glass sheets are used (**Fig. 4.4** and **Fig. 4.5**). The rainscreen reduces the wall depth compared with solid external leaves. In addition, weathered or outdated cladding can be easily replaced. In structural terms this is a single-leaf solid wall with a ventilated cladding. The external appearance of rainscreens can resemble that of a non load-bearing façade, although they have a totally different construction.

So, rainscreen cladding is the attachment of an outer skin of rear-ventilated cladding to a new or existing building. The system is a form of double-wall construction that uses an outer layer to keep out the rain and an inner layer, kept relatively dry, to provide thermal insulation, prevent excessive air leakage and carry wind loading. The outer layer breathes like a skin while the inner layer reduces energy losses. The inner structural leaf can be a concrete or brickwork wall, a cast-concrete wall or a metal-stud wall. A layer of insulation is provided on the outside of the backing wall, finished off with a vapour barrier on the warm side and possible a breather waterproofing membrane on the cold side of the insulation.

Since a rainscreen has no thermal insulation and there is no connection to the building's warm areas, it is sometimes referred to as a cold façade. Rainscreens are always vertical, since the joints between panels are open for ventilation and water penetration would be an issue in sloped walls. Rainscreen cladding is an economic alternative to curtain walls in opaque façades.

Since rainscreen systems overclad the building envelope with opaque units, they can offer a very good opportunity for the integration of PV modules without needing major modification to the existing technology. Rainscreen façades are hung from load-bearing exterior walls and consist of a substructure and its anchoring. The ventilated cavity contained within the system helps to keep down the operating temperatures of the PV cells, thus enhancing performance. It also provides space for cable routes.

Fig. 4.6 An example of a curtain wall system where the exterior walls are not required for structural support.
Photo: David Millington Photography Limited
Courtesy: Arup

4.2.3 Curtain wall systems

The widespread use of structural steel and reinforced concrete allows relatively small columns to support large loads, so the exterior walls of buildings are not required for structural support.

A curtain wall is any exterior wall that is attached to the building structure **(Fig. 4.6)** and which does not carry the floor or roof loads of the building. The load of the curtain wall itself is transferred to the main building structure through connections at floors or columns of the building. A curtain wall is designed to resist air and water infiltration, wind forces acting on the building and its own dead load forces. In seismically active areas, a curtain wall must also resist seismic forces imposed by the inertia of the curtain wall itself.

Curtain walls are also referred to as warm façades because the thermal-insulation layer is applied directly to the surface of the building.
Curtain walls are typically designed with extruded aluminium or steel members. The aluminium frame is usually infilled with glass, which provides an architecturally pleasing building, as well as benefits such as daylighting. However, parameters related to solar gain control, such as thermal comfort and visual comfort, are more difficult to control when using highly glazed curtain walls. Other common infills include: stone veneer, metal panels, louvres and operable windows or vents.

Curtain walls can be designed to span multiple floors. In vertical or sloped walls, curtain walling is a well-known, standard and economical solution.
PV modules can cover the entire surface. From the point of view of performance, the lack of rear ventilation of the PV modules, compared to a rainscreen, can cause a reduction in output. A double-skin façade, described later, is a solution to this, though more expensive and complex.
There are two ways of building a curtain wall:
— the stick system, erected on site
— the unitised system, prefabricated in the factory

4.2.4 Stick system curtain wall

The stick system type of curtain wall using a post-and-rail construction is very popular solution. It is also called mullion-transom stick system.

Stick curtain walling normally comprises vertical structural framing members (mullions) that span from floor to floor and are erected first (Fig. 4.7). These are followed by horizontal transom, which are fixed in-between the mullions.

In the framework are fitted infill units, which may comprise a mixture of fixed and opening glazing and insulated panels, of which these may include metal, painted glass or stone panels.

The infill elements located in a rebate float to some extent, the rebate depth taking into account the tolerances, movements and deformations to be expected.

This form of construction relies heavily on a skilled site workforce since it is assembled on site. Site-based controls would deal with issues such as installation procedures, tolerance, movement joints and sealing of the system. The erection work requires scaffolding, is time-consuming, and delayed in bad weather conditions.

Stick system curtain walls are widely used for low-rise building where a middle- to high-quality cladding system is required. Compared to other curtain walling systems, it presents a lower cost per square metre and a less complex replacement strategy. Since there is a need for scaffold, it is not recommended for high-rise construction.

PV modules can be integrated into stick system curtain walling system, either in the vision area or in the opaque area of the façade. They can be mounted and waterproofed into the façade in the same way as ordinary glass. However the dimension of modules used have to fit the façade exactly so bespoke modules are likely to be required.

Fig. 4.7 An example of site installation of stick system curtain walling.
Photo courtesy: Arup

4.2.5 Unitised system curtain wall

Unitised curtain walling was developed to overcome the problems associated with stick systems of scaffolding, live loads accommodation and long on-site time. It usually comprises storey-height units of steel or aluminium framework, glazing and opaque panels pre-assembled in a factory. They contain all the necessary elements that the external building fabric would require, such as external weathering elements, insulation, vapour barrier, fire protection, beyond the frame members and the infill panels.

This work takes place under controlled, industrial conditions with a high degree of automation and high level of accuracy. This leads to reliable quality assurance measures and hence a consistently high standard of quality. Completely prefabricated façade modules are delivered to the site and hung on adjustable brackets previously fixed to the structure. The installation process is relatively simple and can be carried out from inside the building, therefore eradicating the need of external scaffolding (Fig. 4.8).

Unitised or prefabricated façades require experienced designers and engineers. Mistakes at the design stage cannot easily be corrected by additional manual measures. These façades require more intensive planning and therefore need appropriate planning lead times, something that must be taken into account when awarding contracts. However, they are equally suitable for high-rise buildings and single-storey sheds, and are preferred for those with a regular structural system.

PV modules can be integrated in a unitised system either in the vision area or in the opaque area of the façade. The solar modules can be integrated into prefabricated panels during their assembly in the factory. All penetrations of electrical wiring through the framing members or weather seals can therefore be sealed in the factory conditions with close quality control.

Unitised systems are better from the construction point of view, because the PV installation, weathering and connections are done in the factory under controlled quality conditions. As for the stick system, the dimension of modules have to fit the façade exactly so bespoke modules are likely to be required.

Fig. 4.8 An example of site installation of a unitised system where the façade units are each fitted from inside the building.
Photo courtesy: Arup

4.2.6 Double-skin façade

Many architects—and their clients—prefer buildings with all-glass façades. Many of these use a single-skin façade consisting of fixed glazing (vision panels) that forms the outer surface of the building. Glazing poses less resistance to heat transfer than insulated walls. Therefore compared to buildings with largely opaque façades, highly glazed buildings tend to have greater heating loads in winter and greater cooling loads in summer from heat transfer through the building envelope.

Double-skin façades are sometimes referred to as a "building in a building" (Fig. 4.9). The façade consists of an inner skin separated by a significant amount of air space from the outer skin. These façade systems first came into use in the 1970s in an to attempt to improve the thermal-energy performance of façades of buildings with high glazing fractions.

Between the heat-insulated inner façade and the outer skin is an unheated thermal buffer zone, which is ventilated if required and can incorporate solar shading devices. Air can flow through the cavity via natural or mechanical ventilation and is used to help moderate building thermal loads. Most commonly, outdoor air flows into the bottom of the cavity and exhausts from the top of the cavity outdoors. Double-skin façades are typically used in multi-storey buildings on one or more sides of the building that receive appreciable sun.

The outer façade is extremely suitable for integrating photovoltaics since it often consists of single glazing and the modules can also provide solar shading. Furthermore there is effective ventilation of the back to minimise temperature rise that would otherwise reduce output power.

Fig. 4.9 An example of a double-skin façade, sometimes known as a "building in building".
Photo: Harris Poirazis

4.2.7 Atria and canopies

For the highest BIPV performance, the horizontal facets of a building are the best: free from overshadowing, close to optimal tilt angle, and easy to ventilate. This location is also the preferred option if PV should not alter the building image.

There are many lay-on systems for roof-mounted PV modules. This handbook covers building integration, as necessary for incorporation into skylights over atria and in canopies. The PV integration is visible from inside and the proportion of opaque PV area can be adjusted for the appropriate degree of sunshading.

The control of the inner-space conditions is an important driver when designing an inclined or horizontal envelope, particularly when the percentage of glazed area is high (Fig. 4.10). Heat losses in winter and heat gains in summer can easily increase compared to a plain opaque and insulated roof.

Important issues of this type of construction (especially with small slope) are the risk of condensation in the bottom side of the glass and the accumulation of dirt on the upper glass.

Fig. 4.10 Canopy of the community centre Ludesch (A) with PV modules laminated into the glazing.
Photo courtesy: HEI GmbH

4.2.8 Façade procurement

The façade industry, particularly for curtain walling, has developed as an integral part of the procurement process. Framing members and panels can be supplied in a reasonably short timescale for a wide variety of façade designs ranging from standard to quite complex.
Where bespoke PV modules are selected for use, their impact on the procurement timescale through introducing long lead times must be considered and noted.

The standard stages for a conventional curtain wall are as follows where indicative timescales are given for straightforward designs:
— definition of the final design: at least two weeks
— material supply: three weeks
— finishing off and delivering to site: three weeks

The design stage is the most complex and time consuming. The duration can extend well beyond two weeks depending on the complexity of the proposed design.
Design of the framing members does not play a significant role in terms of timing. Usually they are taken from the catalogue or, even if a bespoke system, their design develops from existing products. The design of the panels can lengthen the time.
In case of simple panels of the same size and shape, the design is quite straightforward and can be fully developed in two weeks. If the building presents a particularly sophisticated geometry with panels of different shapes and sizes, their design can be quite a lengthy process. This is because not only do the geometrical features of the panels need to be defined but also the position and the installation sequence has to be carefully evaluated and planned.
The material supplying stage can involve about three weeks for profiles of the framing members: one week for the order and extrusion process, two weeks for the powder-coating process. For panels with simple geometry, their production can be parallel to manufacturing the framing members and completed in three weeks.
For buildings with a complex geometry, production of the panels can still be quite simple if the geometric variations are limited, but the time will increase in proportion to increase in geometric variations.
Finally all the components reach the contractor's factory where they are cut, finished off and sent to site in case of a stick system, or assembled and sent to site in case of a unitised system.

4.3 Envelope performance requirements

A building façade provides a barrier between the dynamic, often harsh and uncontrolled, external environment and a fairly static and comfortable internal climate. The building envelope needs to manage or prevent the flow of air, water/moisture, heat and sound between these greatly varying environments. In addition, the building façade needs to deal with issues relating to safety and the containment of people within buildings, fire and even vandalism or burglary. These considerations result in a comprehensive set of performance requirements for any given façade design.

The modern wall consists of a series of performance "layers" (**Fig. 4.11**). The purpose of this section is briefly to discuss the various performance requirements for façades.

4.3.1 Design life

The typical design life of building envelopes and their components depends on the building use. For example, normal design life for office buildings is 60 years.
Three types of elements must be considered when discussing the design life of building façades:

— Replaceable elements: elements which are intended to last less than the design life of the building and for which replacement has to be considered at design stage. For example, double-glazed units (20–25 years) and sealants (20–25 years).
— Maintainable elements: elements that are intended to last the design life of the building with periodic treatment and maintenance. For example ironmongery and weathering gaskets.
— Lifelong elements: elements that are intended to last the design life of the building without maintenance. For example, structural bracketry and cladding framing members.

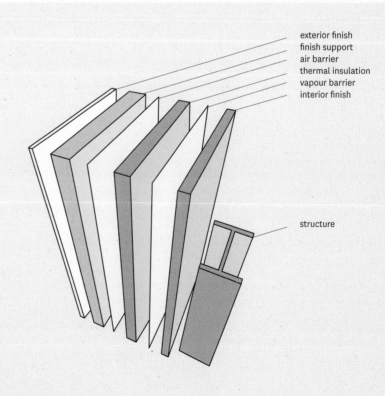

exterior finish
finish support
air barrier
thermal insulation
vapour barrier
interior finish

structure

Fig. 4.11 The modern wall is made up of a series of performance layers. Some materials may perform more than one function and their position in the layer may change according to façade design.
Source: National Institute of Building Sciences: Whole building design guide

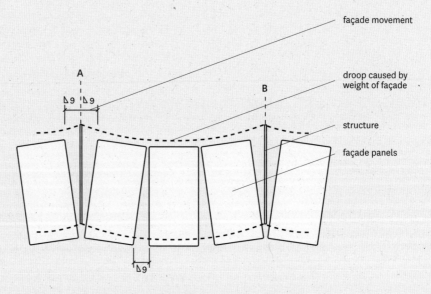

Fig. 4.12 Relationship between structure and façade for gravity movements, as applicable to a stick-system or a unitised-system curtain wall.

façade movement

droop caused by weight of façade

structure

façade panels

4.3.2 Structural performance

The structural members of cladding systems are designed using a typical Ultimate Limit State (maximum stress)—Serviceability Limit State (maximum deflection) approach. In most cases, building envelopes are designed to withstand wind loads, snow loads and imposed loads such as barrier loading, impact loading and loading due to cleaning and maintenance. Bomb blast loading and seismic effects may also need to be considered.

4.3.3 Building movements and tolerances

Particular attention should be paid to the interface of the structural frame with the cladding around the building. The structural engineer and the designers of the building envelope should liaise as early as possible in the design process to establish the effects of the building frame movements and tolerances (**Fig. 4.12, Fig. 4.13**) on the jointing between the building envelope elements and the connections between the building envelope and the building structure.

The stiffness of the perimeter structure determines the need for movement allowance within the cladding system and joint sizes consequently required. In most cases, providing extra stiffness to the structural framing members around the building perimeter limits movements between the different building envelope elements and thus reduces joint sizes. Exceptions are building envelope components that span from column to column, thus avoiding slab-edge deflections or ground-bearing, self-supporting façades.

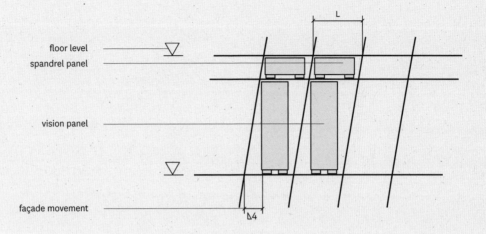

Fig. 4.13 Relationship between structure and façade for sideways movements, as applicable to a stick-system or a unitised-system curtain wall

floor level

spandrel panel

vision panel

façade movement

4.3.4 Air-tightness

The building envelope needs to achieve a certain level of air-tightness to avoid unnecessary space heating and cooling due to infiltration (uncontrolled ventilation) and to enable the effective performance of ventilation systems.

The façade design should incorporate continuous air barriers to minimise air infiltration though the fabric. The air-tightness of a building envelope is expressed by the air permeability which is the volume of air (m^3) that penetrates through a unit of area (m^2) over a unit of time (h) at a given pressure difference (Pa) between the internal and external environment.

4.3.5 Weather-tightness

A building façade needs to be weather-tight. Cladding design should incorporate multiple lines of defence against water ingress. Seals are usually made using pre-formed (extruded) gaskets (EPDM, silicone) and silicone adhesive.

Most cladding systems with drained and ventilated cavities make use of the principle of pressure equalisation to create a weather-tight barrier. A final air-tight seal at the back is essential for the pressure in the chamber to equalise and further assures the weather-tightness of the system, possibly assisted by an additional water seal as second line of defence. It is, however, of utmost importance that all cavities inside a cladding system are drained and ventilated to allow potential water ingress to be guided to the outside.

Testing the weather-tightness of a cladding system is usually done off-site on a performance mock-up under controlled (static or dynamic) pressure conditions. In addition, on-site hose tests can be carried out to establish the quality of workmanship, which can have a critical impact on the weather-tightness of cladding systems in most instances.

4.3.6 Thermal performance

A building envelope needs to mediate the transfer of heat between the internal and external environment. The objective is to create a comfortable indoor environment while using the minimum amount of natural resources (energy).
In climates with pronounced winter and summer seasons, a façade has to deal with changing directions of the resultant heat flow through the façade between winter and summer time conditions.

In winter, the aim is to limit the heat loss through the façade to the outside. The heat loss through a façade is characterised by its thermal transmittance or U-value $(W/(m^2 \cdot K))$. The U-value quantifies the amount of heat which passes through a unit of area (m^2) per unit of time $(W = J/s)$ per unit of temperature difference (K) between the environments on the two sides of a façade. The lower the U-value of the façade elements, the less heat is lost through the building skin.
For simple layered constructions, the overall U-value of a façade can be obtained by easy hand calculations. More complex constructions involving the use of highly conductive metal components (such as curtain walls) however, require more advanced computer calculation methods. Software based on numerical analysis is used to analyse the 2D or 3D (Fig. 4.14, Fig. 4.15) interaction of different façade components and to evaluate the overall thermal performance of cladding systems.

In summer, the aim is to control solar gains entering the building through the façade. Depending on the building type and use, solar gains may be welcome or unwanted. For example, office buildings already have such high internal heat gains due to occupancy levels and office equipment that additional heat gains due to solar radiation should be reduced as much as possible. Residential buildings in contrast may benefit from solar heat gains to reduce space heating in wintertime. However, summer time overheating should be avoided in any building type.

Solar gains mainly occur through the glazed areas of building façades. Solar gains through glazing units are quantified by the total solar energy transmission (solar factor) or g-value. The g-value of a glass build-up is the ratio of the total solar energy flux entering the building through the glazing (W/m^2) to the incident solar energy flux (W/m^2). The total energy is the sum of the incoming solar energy by direct transmission and the energy re-radiated, conducted and convected by the glass to the inside environment after being absorbed by the glazing system.

Fig. 4.14 2D image from numerical analysis of the thermal performance in a curtain wall system. This is a corner detail which is always critical from a thermal point of view.

Fig. 4.15 3D image from numerical analysis of thermal performance in a curtainwall system. This detail shows that the thermal conductance is well broken

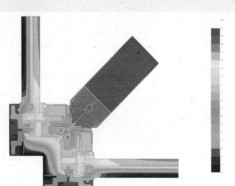

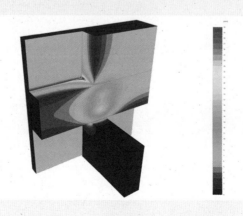

4.3.7 Acoustic performance

The acoustic performance of curtain walls is primarily a function of the glazing mass and composition, and the quality of the internal seals to stop air leakage. Sound insulation of curtain walls can be improved by installing sound attenuating infill and making construction as airtight as possible (Fig. 4.16).

The main parameters to control the acoustic performance of a glazed wall are:
— glass thickness
— air infiltration
— type of glass (annealed, laminated, etc.)
— type of spacer
— insulating glass films
— air space between glass lites (individual raw sheets of glass)
— type of gas fill
— edge effects
— glass size

4.3.8 Fire safety

Precautions are essential to slow the passage of fire and combustion gases between floors. They include fire safing, a fire stop material in the space between floor slab and curtain wall, and smoke seal at gaps between the floors and the back of the curtain wall. Spandrel areas must have non-combustible insulation at the interior face of the curtain wall.
Fire fighting knock-out glazing panels are often required for venting and emergency access from the exterior. Knock-out panels are generally fully tempered glass to allow full fracturing of the panel into small pieces and relatively safe removal from the opening.

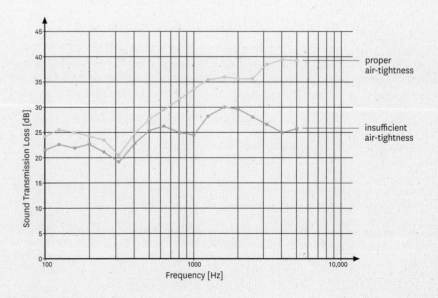

Fig. 4.16 Acoustic performance of a window under conditions of either proper or insufficient airtightness. The example is a single hung window with insulating glass (6 mm annealed, 9 mm air, 5 mm annealed). The insufficient condition is as-received with OITC of 24 and STC of 26. The completely sealed case has OITC 27 and STC 31.
OITC is Outdoor-Indoor Transmission Class, a standard used for indicating the rate of transmission of sound between outdoor and indoor spaces. STC is Sound Transmission Class, an integer rating of how well a building partition attenuates airborne sound.

4.3.9 Glass thermal stress

Thermal stress is the term used to describe the internal stresses created when glass is subjected to variations in temperature across its area.

Glass in the vision and non-vision areas of a façade expands in response to the heat of the sun. The more absorbent the glass, the greater and quicker its response will be to solar radiation. The edges of the glass, however, may be encased within the rebate of the frame and are therefore protected from the direct heat of the sun, thus heating up more slowly and expanding less. Similar effects can occur due to shadows from adjacent features, cast across the glass surface.

If the safe temperature difference between the main area of the glass and the edges is exceeded, the glass may crack.

Thermal breakage is generally recognised by the fact that it starts perpendicular to the edge of the glass and results in a "lazy/meandering" crack. Other factors that affect thermal safety include the presence of blinds, internal heat sources, external shading and geographic location.

When a risk of thermal breakage exists, glass must be heat-treated to ensure thermal safety. Heat-treated glasses include heat-strengthened and toughened glass.

4.3.10 Safety

The integration of PVs with the building should be considered in terms of construction and access for maintenance, in the normal way. For instance in compliance with the CDM (Construction Design and Management) Regulations.

Safety is a standard consideration with all electrical installations. Contact with the front surfaces of PV modules poses no danger but there are particular issues that apply to PV installations:

— Current is produced during a wide variety of light conditions. (PV modules can only be "switched off" by covering with something opaque.)
— There is less familiarity within the building industry with DC compared with AC.
— Voltages can be higher than the familiar 230 V single-phase AC.

Safety issues should be well documented for both installers and maintenance personnel.

4.3.11 Component failure and security

During the lifetime of a building, façade components may fail prematurely due to various reasons:
— accidental damage
— material failure
— vandalism
— bomb blast (**Fig. 4.17, Fig. 4.18**)

Normal safety considerations for glazed façades include containment of occupants and protection of both occupants and people outside the building when a pane of glass is broken.

When designing vertical or horizontal (overhead) glazing, the following issues need to be considered:
— falling people or objects impacting on the glazing
— usage of the space and likelihood of accidental impact
— consequences of glass failure in terms of containment of people and objects and retention of broken glass
— safety issues relating to maintenance and cleaning
— replacement of glazing elements

A current safety concern associated with toughened glass is the risk of spontaneous breakage due to nickel sulphide (NiS) inclusions. Nickel sulphide inclusions occur during the manufacturing process for float glass. During the toughening process, these inclusions change in size from what is known as a low-temperature structure to a high-temperature, crystalline structure. When cooled quickly, the NiS particle is unable to change back to its original form. Over a certain period of time NiS will slowly convert to the original form phase with an increase in volume of about 2–4%. Such increase of NiS may cause glass breakage. The breakage process can continue over a number of years and can raise major safety concerns because of its unpredictability.
To reduce the possibility of breakage from nickel sulphide inclusions in the field, accelerated exposures at high temperatures are conducted in a "heat soak test". The inclusions transform at a rapid rate during the test thereby causing failure before installation of the pane on site. The accelerated exposure or heat soak test reduces but cannot eliminate the likelihood of breakage on site.

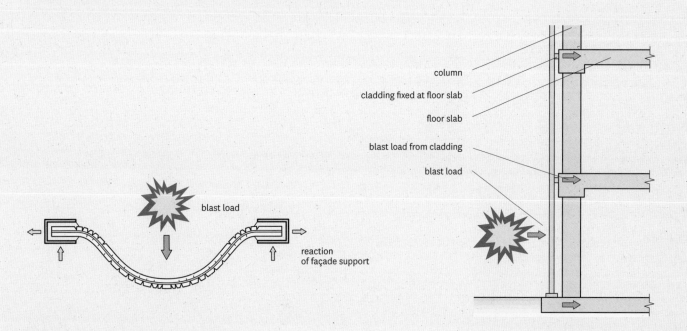

Fig. 4.17 Schematic showing the force transmission of a blast through a laminated glass window.

Fig. 4.18 Schematic showing the force transmission of a blast through the cladding into the main structure.

4.4 PV maintenance

After the PV has been commissioned, maintenance of PV modules is not essential, but implementing a maintenance schedule has benefits. It ensures that the PV array is working at the best performance and alerts if a fault occurs so that corrective action can be taken.

Here is a recommended maintenance schedule:
— On a monthly basis, check and record the electric output.
— Once per year, visually inspect the array.
— Once per year, clean the array as necessary to remove soiling.

A PV array has several electrical parts, all of which must function together efficiently. In the very first BIPV systems, inverters were the main source of electrical problems but their design has matured to high levels of reliability. Furthermore they have useful features, such as recording electrical parameters and logging errors.
Electrical problems can range from open circuit in a module or corrosion in a connection to an inverter failing to generate an AC output. These might show as reduced monthly output from a value typical for the time of year.

The impact of soiling is strongly site-dependent. Where it does occur, it is an important cause of loss output even approaching 10%. Rain provides a good degree of cleaning, washing dust, pollen and similar debris away. Sticky dirt, like bird droppings or exhaust fumes from a heating system, might stay even during severe rainstorms. Similarly once lichen has established, it can only be removed manually. The most critical part of a module is the lower edge where soiling at the edge of the frame occurs, especially with low inclinations (tilt less than 30° from horizontal). Often by repeated water collection in the shallow puddle between the frame and the glass and consecutive evaporation, dirt can accumulate. Over time sufficient dirt might collect to allow plant growth. Once soiling causes shading of the cells, the available power from a module is reduced.
PV modules with little distance between the cells and the lower frame edge are especially of concern. Generally, soiling is a reversible effect and this effect can be resolved by yearly manual cleaning. Laminates allow free run-off of the water so are less prone to this effect.
Close inspection of the array can spot other problems. Examples are failure of a module through de-lamination, physical damage from an impact or lighting damage.

4.5 Array wiring

PV modules often have junction boxes on their back surface that have space for connections and may contain bypass diodes. More usually in BIPV, there are flying leads ready for connection by plug-and-socket into other leads.
The modules are normally linked by "daisy chains". That is, cables loop in to one module and then out to another. Cables join the PV components together and as for any electrical installation they need to be suitable for their environment and for the loads carried. Where cables are run in areas subject to heat build-up at the rear of modules, their size will need to be increased to allow for the higher temperatures. Similarly, if cables are run where water vapour can enter, such as in a rainscreen cladding, the cables, cable ways and junction boxes must be suitably selected.
Routes should be as short as practical to facilitate installation and to minimise cost and voltage drop. The numerous cables involved obviously need to be considered carefully to avoid detracting from final appearance. This is a particularly important issue with PV cladding systems and also where arrays are semi-transparent.
Cables should generally be inaccessible to occupants but accessible to maintenance personnel.

5. SHADING SYSTEMS

5.1 General

Architects strive to improve the comfort of building occupants with respect to day-light and views to the outside. The result is large vision areas in façades, but these can have excessive solar gains. Shading devices are a passive way to limit this effect rather than increase the use of air conditioning. External shading also provides a powerful visual statement. Architects are increasingly seeing external shading in a positive way so that it is becoming established in architectural expression. External shades can be fixed or adjustable, metal or glass, large or small and can also be incorporated into maintenance walkway systems. The term louvres refers to adjustable and fixed shading devices.

5.2 Principles of construction

External louvres, both horizontal and vertical, are used on many buildings (**Fig. 5.1**). Louvres can be mounted close or at a distance to the window and some are made retractable for cleaning.

Louvres are fixed back with bracketry either simply to the cladding frame or directly to the building structure through penetrations in the cladding. The method used depends on their size, weight and offset with respect to the façade.

The main issues concerning external louvres are their resistance to wind loading, noise and vibration caused by wind, durability, and maintenance and cleaning of louvres and the façade. Moveable blinds can be manually operated or by a Building Management System (BMS) provided with manual override by building occupants. Some external shading elements cannot withstand maximum wind loading in certain positions, so they are closed or retracted automatically by the BMS in case of high winds. Larger and more robust external shading systems are often integrated in to a system of external walkways hanging off the primary façade, which provides access for cleaning and maintenance.

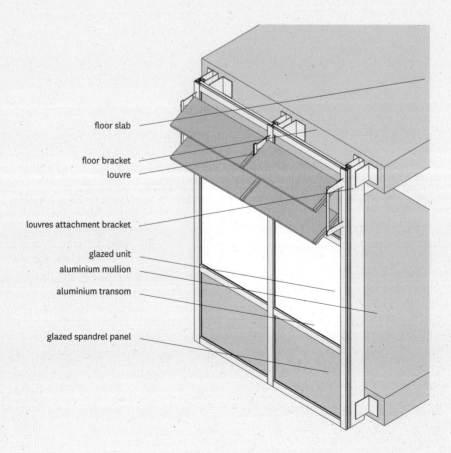

floor slab

floor bracket

louvre

louvres attachment bracket

glazed unit

aluminium mullion

aluminium transom

glazed spandrel panel

Fig. 5.1 General features of a curtain wall with louvres.

5.3 Integration of PV modules

There are good opportunities to combine PV modules into shading devices in contemporary buildings (Fig. 5.3). The use of PV modules as shading features gives tangible expression of conserving energy through both reduced cooling loads and utilising solar energy.

PV modules could be readily substituted for the external blinds in metal, timber or plastic materials now used, but would probably be too fragile to retract unless mounted in a protective frame.

It is important to avoid overshadowing between louvres at times when there is good solar generating potential (when the sun is more square-on rather than oblique). Careful shadowing analysis should be carried out with 3D software. Alternatively use single large louvres for each window row rather than several shallow louvres.

A promising option for PV louvres is to mount them some distance from the window and incorporate them in to a walkway system, which would provide access for cleaning and maintenance (Fig. 5.2).

Some louvres systems are intended to be turned automatically to provide maximum shade, matching the angle of the sun. Where PV is integrated, the power for this operation would only be necessary when the sun is shining, and thus, in principle, could be derived from the PV modules themselves.

Large sun-shades offer another opportunity to use PV modules in a positive manner. They would be used to shade an entire storey of a building, or even two or three storeys. They too could incorporate walkways for maintenance and cleaning, and could incorporate PV modules into the shade itself.

The bracketry and supporting framework for the shading elements can be suitable to guide the wiring, both to connect modules and to channel the wiring from an array to the inside of the building. The design should enable all wiring in the wet zone to follow drained and ventilated channels. Wiring should be brought together in a number of central locations to minimise the penetrations of the cladding line when entering the building. See also canopies in Chapter 10.

Fig. 5.2 Maintenance access for the PV louvres at Caltrans Building in Los Angeles (USA).
Photo: Roland Halbe
Courtesy: Arup

Fig. 5.3 Inside detail of glass-glass laminated PV as louvres at Caltrans Building in Los Angeles (USA).
Photo: Jim Sinsheimer
Courtesy: Arup

5.4 Maintenance & replacement

PV modules are mainly suitable for integration into larger, more robust louvres and shading systems. These shading systems often incorporate external walkways or grilles specifically designed for cleaning and maintenance. As such, the design of the integrated PV system should encompass direct access to the modules, fixings, junction boxes and associated wiring.

The design should also consider the cleaning strategy of the PV modules, either by direct access from the walkways or by a rotating mechanism which allows the exposed surfaces of the shading elements to be cleaned from the walkways.

The walkways may also be designed to withstand the imposed loads from shading element- or glazing-unit replacement. Particular attention should be paid to the glass-replacement strategy as the shading system can obstruct direct access to and replacement of the glazing units from outside.

Since electric wiring is likely to be incorporated into the walkways, the design of the system should provide sufficient protection and allow easy inspection and maintenance operations.

Fig. 5.4 PV louvres at an office building in Neustrelitz (D).
Photo courtesy: Schüco International KG

5.5 Case study:
Galleria Naviglio

Location

Town, country: Faenza, Italy
Latitude, longitude, elevation: 44.313°, 11.898°, 23 m
Average horizontal irradiation: 3.82 kWh/(m²·day)

PV

Area: 285 m²
Peak power specification: 23 kW$_P$
Power output: 33,345 kWh/y estimate
Individual module dimensions:
1937 & 2200 × 299 mm
Technology: monocrystalline silicon
Manufacturer: Schüco

Building

Type: office, shops & apartments
Height, storeys: 11 m, 4
Floor area: 4000 m²
Architects: Studio Technico
Completed: 2003

5.5.1 Background

The Galleria Naviglio complex consists of two buildings totalling 4000 m² for offices, shops and apartments. The complex is in an area of Italy where green building design is encouraged through such measures as grants and permission for a larger building size than normal.

Within the area designated for the green design strategy, there is a central cogeneration plant for simultaneous generation of heat and electrical energy. A district heating net has been installed which the new complex connects to for heating and cooling for each flat, the retail area and the offices.

Additional green design features on the complex are green roofing for much of the horizontal roof surface, and BIPV in the shading (Fig. 5.6).

5.5.2 Construction

The two buildings use a reinforced-concrete structure to meet anti-seismic requirements. The infill panels on the north façades are precast-concrete panels with an external visible brick wall. The south, east and west elevations use a curtain walling system, preferred for the wider glazed surfaces. External glass louvres are used on the lightweight elevations on the southeast, northeast and southwest faces to provide some level of protection from the solar radiation. These louvres are fitted with monocrystalline silicon PV cells (Fig. 5.5). The PV louvres are tilted 70° from horizontal and cover a surface of 285 m². The array specification is 23 kW$_P$.

Fig. 5.5 Detail of the external PV louvres on the Galleria Naviglio. Transmission of light between the cells is evident in the reflection in the façade of the bottom row.
Photo courtesy: Schüco International KG

Fig. 5.6 Curtain walling façade with external PV louvres. View onto the south face.
Photo courtesy: Schüco International KG

6. RAINSCREEN SYSTEMS

6.1 General

Rainscreen over-cladding adopts a two-stage approach to weather resistance whereby the rain and wind barriers are separated by an air-space cavity. The outer leaf acting as rainscreen provides the major barrier to rain penetration, while the inner leaf of the wall, which forms the air barrier, is kept relatively dry.

The inner structural leaf or backing wall can be built of any material, for example concrete or brickwork, a cast-concrete wall or a metal-stud wall. A layer of insulation is provided on the outside of the backing wall, finished off with a vapour barrier on the warm side (on the inside in a typical central-Europe climate) and possibly a breather-type waterproofing membrane on the cold side of the insulation (on the outside in a typical central-Europe climate).

Vertical cladding rails or fixing brackets are bolted on to the backing wall ready to receive the outer rainscreen panels **(Fig. 6.1)**. The outer screen, together with a thought-through drainage and ventilation system, protects the inner leaf from the deleterious effects of heavy wetting and solar radiation, so the effects of thermal expansion and contraction are minimised. The outer sleeve also serves as a cosmetic element to the building envelope.

In addition to new buildings, rainscreens are widely used as replacement or remediation for old, low-performing envelopes. The complete refurbishment process can be carried out without empting the building.

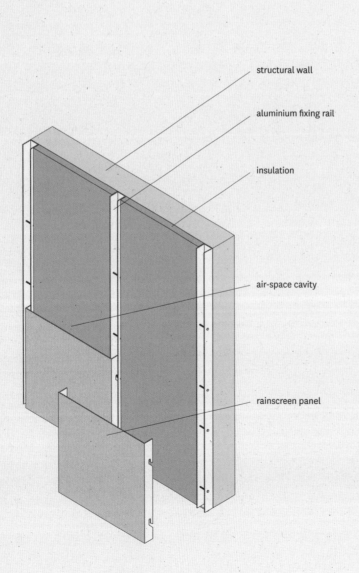

Fig. 6.1 General scheme of a rainscreen cladding system in front of an opaque wall.

structural wall

aluminium fixing rail

insulation

air-space cavity

rainscreen panel

Fig. 6.2 Vertical section through a typical horizontal joint detail in a drained and back-ventilated metal rainscreen.

Fig. 6.3 Vertical section through a typical horizontal joint detail in a pressure-equalised rainscreen.

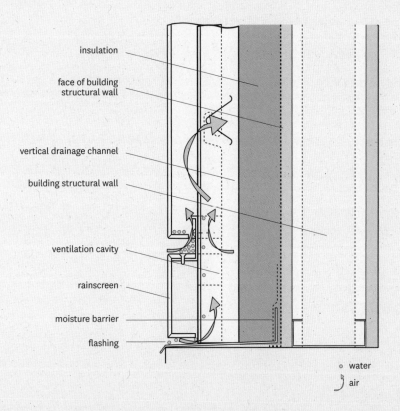

insulation

face of building
structural wall

vertical drainage channel

building structural wall

ventilation cavity

rainscreen

moisture barrier

flashing

○ water

air

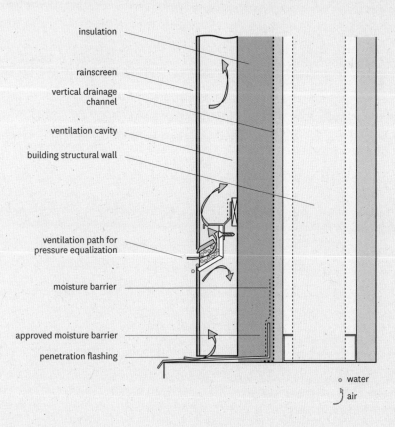

insulation

rainscreen

vertical drainage
channel

ventilation cavity

building structural wall

ventilation path for
pressure equalization

moisture barrier

approved moisture barrier

penetration flashing

○ water

air

6.2 Principles of construction

There are two variations of the rainscreen system: the "drained and back-ventilated" rainscreen and the "pressure-equalised" rainscreen. The difference between the two systems is the amount of water that is permitted into the cavity.

In the drained and back-ventilated rainscreen (**Fig. 6.2**), no deliberate attempt is made to prevent water ingress through the joints, and relatively large quantities of rain penetrate the joints and run down the reverse side of the cladding panel. This water is allowed to drain and evaporate from the cavity.

In the pressure-equalised system (**Fig. 6.3**), water penetration is controlled by the use of baffles, compartmentation, drips, upstands, barriers and opening sizes in the assembly, in order to equalise the pressure in the cavity with the external pressure. This results in reducing the force of rain, dispersion of moisture behind the outer leaf and only minor leakage into the cavity. Positive drainage and ventilation are still provided however to remove this water. Moreover the barriers act as fire protection hampering the chimney effect within the cavity.

Both are constructed using a lightweight metal rainscreen panel, usually coated aluminium. Other options are stone, terracotta and concrete panels. This is fixed to the primary structure using bolts, studs or purpose-designed cladding rails. If a hook-on system is used, additional mechanical fixings are required to lock panels in place to prevent panels from coming loose due to uplift.

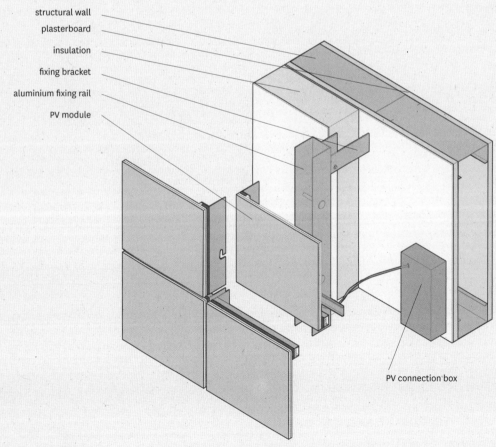

structural wall
plasterboard
insulation
fixing bracket
aluminium fixing rail
PV module

PV connection box

Fig. 6.4 Detail of a rainscreen panel integrated with a PV module showing electrical connections.

72

6. RAINSCREEN SYSTEMS

6.3 Integration of PV modules

Rainscreen over-cladding systems offer a very good opportunity for the integration of PV modules (Fig. 6.4). In the case of existing cladding technology, no major modification would be needed to incorporate solar modules. Furthermore the ventilated cavity contained within the system would help to keep the operating temperatures of the PV cells down to some degree.

The lightweight metal panels of a standard rainscreen could be modified to receive PV modules. The metal panels could be adapted to form a frame into which the modules can be fixed. The edges of solar modules can be framed with aluminium extrusions/stainless steel channels along two or four sides and fixed back to cladding rails or proprietary brackets.

The junction box could be located on the back of the solar rainscreen panels depending on the cavity width and the allocated cladding zone. The wiring would be located behind the rainscreen panels, far from the wet zone, and could be guided along the vertical (drained and ventilated) tracks used to mount the panels to the backing wall. The cabling could be brought together at the base of the wall to enter the building through one carefully detailed penetration of the external envelope.

To limit the presence of water behind the rainscreen panel, it is suggested that a pressure-equalised rainscreen system represents the best opportunity for PV integration.

A rainscreen is normally dimensioned against the floor heights of the building and window spacing. The resulting grid dictates the dimensions of the lightweight metal panels. Bespoke PV modules can be used but these specially made laminates will add expense.

Using standard off-the-shelf PV modules keeps the cost down but has implications for the dimensions of the rainscreen grid. In some types of rainscreen, the grid dimensions can be adjusted to suit the modules, as in the plain wall without windows shown in Fig. 8.2. Another example is The Co-operative Insurance Tower, shown later in this chapter, which is free from the constraints of windows, for instance. Off-the-shelf modules can also be used in a rainscreen where the module dimensions can be accommodated to a degree. An example of this is the Northumberland Building case study (see Chapter 12 on Refurbishment). The module height fits well with the height of the overhang while the repeat width of the modules does not need to align with the windows.

6.4 Maintenance & replacement

A PV façade can be left without cleaning since rain water running down provides washing of the modules to a degree (**Fig. 6.5**). In some local conditions, rain carries enough dirt to leave a residue which will reduce power output. Therefore the cleaning regime for the PV façade should be the same as would be used for any glass or metal façade on the building.

Where a standard cleaning cradle running on a track along the perimeter of the roof is available, the PV modules can be cleaned. Such a dedicated cleaning system can sometimes provide access to the modules for maintenance and replacement, as long as the size and weight of the module are limited. Usually a cradle can only support up to 250 kg, so for large and heavy modules, a dedicated replacement strategy, as for typical curtain walling, needs to be applied.

Maintenance and replacement of solar modules would be fairly easy since all PV components can be accessed from outside. Individual modules could be dismantled quickly by unlocking the fixing brackets. De-mounting of an individual or series of modules gains access to the wiring.

Fig. 6.5 PV integration in a rainscreen on
Manchester College of Art & Technology.
Photo: Daniel Hopkinson
Courtesy: Arup

6.5 Case study: The Co-operative Insurance Tower

Location

Town, country: Manchester, UK
Latitude, longitude, elevation: 53.487°, −2.238°, 54 m
Average horizontal irradiation: 2.53 kWh/(m²·day)

PV

Area: 3972 m²
Peak power specification: 391 kW$_p$
Power output: 183,000 kWh/y
Individual module dimensions:
1200 × 530 mm
Technology: polycrystalline silicon
Manufacturer: Sharp
Completed: 2006

Building

Type: office, conference, cinema
Height, storeys: 118 m, 25
Floor area: 54,000 m²
Architects: Heritage Architecture Ltd.

6.5.1 Background

The Co-operative Insurance Tower is a 28-storey, office building in central Manchester, UK (Fig. 6.6). Built in 1962 to provide new premises for The Co-operative Insurance, the Tower has been dominating the city's skyline for over 40 years. The building comprises three distinct elements: a podium at the base, office accommodation with glazed aluminium curtain walling and a windowless concrete service tower on the south-west side.

The architects for the original 1960s design were GS Hay of the CWS and Gordon Tait of Sir John Burnet, Tait and Partners. They decided to clad the concrete service tower with 14 million mosaic tesserae or tiles each 20 × 20 mm, to create a "shimmering and sparkling column" (Fig. 6.10). The Tower is located on the northern boundary to the city of Manchester and represents a striking symbol and a gateway upon entering the city from the north. The building is categorised as Grade II listed ("a building of special architectural or historic interest" within England and Wales). The mosaic tiles were stuck directly onto the concrete structure, but lacking a movement or expansion joint, tension stresses appeared in the grout between the concrete structure and the mosaic cladding. For most of the building's life, numbers of tiles have been regularly separating from the building envelope (Fig. 6.11). An innovative approach to this façade problem was needed and the eventual solution was to clad the failing mosaic with PV modules forming a rainscreen. The resulting PV array could also contribute to reducing the building's reliance on grid electricity through generation of about 180 MWh/y.

Fig. 6.6 View from the south onto the service tower of The Co-operative Insurance Tower showing the completed PV cladding.
Photo: David Millington Photography Limited
Courtesy: Arup

6.5.2 Why a PV array?

In 2003, increasing concerns about the safety issue of falling tiles prompted search for a solution. Three possible options were identified:

1. Replace with new mosaics throughout, installing these with stress/expansion joints. The replacement material would be similar to the original so the appearance would have been impacted only by the introduction of the new joints. However removing all the old tiles would be lengthy, noisy and costly.

2. Remove all the mosaics and paint or render the bare surface. Although the lowest cost option, this would have met serious problems with the Grade II listing of the exterior, since it would have fundamentally and negatively impacted the appearance of the building.

3. Overclad to retain the mosaics while awaiting developments in technology for fixing mosaics to concrete. This approach offered a high degree of certainty as a solution since the existing mosaic finish could remain conserved beneath the cladding. The appearance would be different but there was an opportunity to achieve a high quality and lasting aesthetic result. Also there would be the opportunity to design in provision for future maintenance.

If option 3 of overcladding was to be pursued, there was concern over the nature and appearance of the cladding material given the listed status. The option to use PV was going to be challenging but could provide the opportunity to make a difference in using new materials and generating renewable energy with reduced emissions.

The Co-operative Insurance are a company with an ethos for corporate social responsibility, encouraging its managers to include environmental issues as a priority in their thinking and plans. Therefore the concept of generating some of the building's energy using renewables technology was seen by them as a priority. Concerning the appearance, the planning authority of the City Council accepted that the PV modules could make a very special effect but insisted that the massive monolithic appearance of the service tower needed to be maintained. English Heritage were consulted and they gave listed-building consent for the change.

Fig. 6.7 Close-up of some polycrystalline silicon modules that are assembled into a cassette. This appearance contrasts noticeably with the coated-steel dummy panels at the bottom.
Photo: David Millington Photography Limited
Courtesy: Arup

6.5.3 Choice of PV technology

In the first assessment, thin-film technology appeared to represent an aesthetically suitable cladding material. The modules are a lower cost than crystalline silicon modules. Moreover, standard thin-film modules are available in a variety of sizes. However the planning authority raised concerns about the appearance of the thin-film modules on the building. The overall effect would have been too uniform, losing existing identification of the floor-to-floor separation of 3.74 m, a key feature in the original mosaic design.

Polycrystalline modules have a more desirable appearance. Furthermore the size of standard modules available from Sharp overcame the planners aesthetic concerns **(Fig. 6.8)**. The particular module was the Sharp NE-8E2E, 1200 mm wide by 530 mm high with a frame thickness of 35 mm. A "cassette" formed of seven modules could be created in which the cassette height of 3.71 m corresponded to the floor-to-floor separation required by the planning authority.

The cassette width of 1.20 m means that the wide south façade and narrow east and west façades are incompletely covered, yet an absolutely even appearance was essential. Electrically inactive PV modules with a bespoke width of 230 mm were used for the visible areas **(Fig. 6.7)**. For less prominent parts, plain blue powder-coated steel panels sufficed.

Fig. 6.8 View onto the north west corner showing three types of cladding. There are cassettes of seven PV modules which are electrically active. The narrower PV modules along the corners have identical appearance but are electrically inactive. Inexpensive coated steel dummy panels are used around the vent because this location on the façade is virtually out of sight from the ground.
Photo: Tom Swailes

6.5.4 Façade engineering

The rainscreen used for the cladding is a pressure-equalised type. The wall is concrete so installation of the rainscreen was mostly concerned with mounting the PV modules.

Before installing the photovoltaic modules, a metal mesh was fixed over the mosaic for retention (Fig. 6.13). Aluminium mullions run the full height of the tower and were fixed to the concrete structure by brackets (Fig. 6.9). Seven photovoltaic modules were joined vertically together by aluminium framing members to form each cassette. The cassettes then slot onto the full height mullions, which also incorporate restraint for the maintenance cradle when in operation.

Installation was designed to be carried out by a series of "mast climbers" around the service tower. These are continuous platforms used to fix the restraining mesh, supporting brackets and mullions. PV cassettes where placed onto the platforms, taken to the required level and lifted into position. The cassettes used a bolted connection that was slotted in.

The floor-to-floor feature seen from afar required a vertical joint between cassettes of 75 mm. This coincided conveniently with the height of the hanging slot connection allowing any cassette to be removed at a later date.

The design incorporated a roof-mounted maintenance cradle. Stability for the cradle is achieved using shuttles fixed to the cradle that run down the mullions. In the event of a damaged module needing to be replaced, the maintenance cradle can take a replacement cassette to the required point, remove the cassette with the damaged module and fit the replacement cassette. The damaged cassette can then be taken to the ground where it can be easily dismantled and the damaged module removed and sent for repair or replaced.

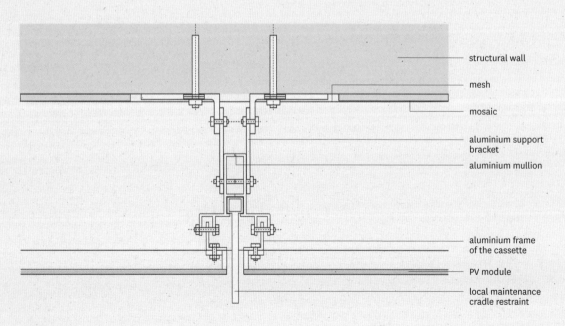

structural wall

mesh

mosaic

aluminium support bracket

aluminium mullion

aluminium frame of the cassette

PV module

local maintenance cradle restraint

Fig. 6.9 Cross-section of the bracket fixing system for attaching cassettes of PV modules to the wall of The Co-operative Insurance Tower.

6.5.5 Electrical

Each cassette of seven modules was connected in series, and three cassettes were joined to make a string operating at about 360 V DC. Each string was connected back to a DC insolator by a pair of double-insulated, single-core cables. These were inserted in a cable tray, attached to the cladding support structure and mounted within the 25 mm zone defined by the angles retaining the mesh.

The DC insolators are sized to enable the DC supply into the inverter to be safely disconnected, even under full-load conditions.

Inverters take the DC power generation from the series-connected strings of PV modules and convert it to useful AC power for use within the building. The three sides of the service tower receive very different irradiance in direct sun conditions. A range of different-sized PV inverters was used to match the layout of PV modules and to ensure that the array is producing the maximum amount of AC power possible at any time of the day.

The output from each inverter was routed into an AC distributor sub-panel and then above the main lift lobbys false ceiling and into the pilot busbar riser cupboard at each floor level. There are six main points of PV system AC output connection into the building's existing AC distributor system.

6.5.6 Performance display

As part of the communication aspect, a large-format display unit was installed in the main foyer of the building (Fig. 6.12). This provided live information to staff and visitors on: power output (kW), total amount of energy generated to date (kWh) and amount of CO_2 emissions offset by the PV generation.

Fig. 6.10 The Co-operative Insurance Tower in its original form before PV integration. This view is from the south east showing two sides of the mosaic-clad service tower to the left of the office accommodation.
Photo courtesy: Arup

Fig. 6.11 Close-up of the mosaics on The Co-operative Insurance Tower before PV integration, showing the damaged areas.
Photo courtesy: Arup

Fig. 6.12 The large-format display used in the main foyer of The Cooperative Insurance Tower to demonstrate the performance of the PV system.
Photo: David Millington Photography Limited
Courtesy: Arup

Fig. 6.13 First stage of PV integration of The Co-operative Insurance Tower showing retaining mesh over the original mosaic and a bracket securing an aluminium mullion. Also shown is the cable tray for module-connection wiring.
Photo courtesy: Arup

6.6 Case study:
Xicui Entertainment Complex

Location

Town, country: Beijing, P.R. China
Latitude, longitude, elevation: 39.905°, 116.277°, 62 m
Average horizontal irradiation: 4.32 kWh/(m²·day)

PV

Area: 534 m²
Peak power specification: 79 kW$_P$
Power output: 38,929 kWh/y
Individual module dimensions:
890 × 890 mm
Technology: polycrystalline silicon
Manufacturer: Sunways, Schüco & Suntech
Completed: 2008

Building

Type: mixed development
Height, storeys: 12 m, 9
Floor area: 2200 m²
Architects: Simone Giostra & Partners Inc.

6.6.1 Background

The Xicui Entertainment Complex is a nine-storey building located in the western part of Beijing, close to some of the 2008 Olympic Games sport facilities. The building was completed in 2005 to house a movie theatre and high-quality restaurant. In 2006 the metal cladding on the east façade was replaced with a 60 × 33 m curtain wall designed by Simone Giostra Architects with support from Arup (Fig. 6.16).
The client desired an interesting, innovative and exciting façade design to enliven his building. Simone Giostra Architects and Arup responded with an "organic solution" made of translucent PV modules and light emitting diodes (LEDs).

Fig. 6.14 An example lighting pattern at night of the
LED array on the Xicui Entertainment Complex.
Photo: Frank P. Palmer
Courtesy: Simone Giostra & Partners/Arup

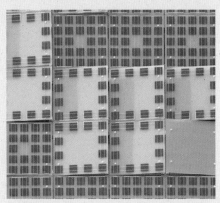

Fig. 6.15 Three different types of glass laminate PV modules containing zero, twelve or twenty-four PV cells.
Photo: Frank P. Palmer
Courtesy: Simone Giostra & Partners/Arup

Fig. 6.16 View onto the south-east corner of the Xicui Entertainment Complex partway through installation of the PV and LED facade on the east side.
Photo: Frank P. Palmer
Courtesy: Simone Giostra &Partners/Arup

6.6.2 Why PV?

Through the concept of an "organic solution", the architects wanted to develop a façade which could generate light from the same energy absorbed by the façade itself. They also wanted it to interact with the building's internal environment and the outer public space.

This vertical cladding consists of translucent glazed modules with a variable density of PV cells to provide an engaging pattern during the day. About 2300 LEDs are fitted behind the translucent glazing making it the largest LED wall in the world at this time (Fig. 6.14).

During the day, the energy produced by the PV cells that is not required for the activities of the building is exported to the grid. During the night the media envelope "takes" the earlier generated energy back to put through the LED in the form of "bursting light".

6.6.3 PV-modules

The key elements of the façade are open-joint laminated glass modules 890× 890 mm (Fig. 6.19) with embedded polycrystalline PV cells and bolt-fixed to the cladding structure. To increase the variety of sunlight reflections on the façade during daytime, half of the glass modules have a 5° tilt outward to left or right.

The PV cells are laminated between two glass panels using an adhesive interlayer which has been treated in order to provide a translucent diffusive appearance. During the day, sufficient daylight passes through openings on the backing wall so that a high level of comfort can be achieved inside the building in terms of quality of the light. From the outside, the diffusive effect of the interlayer is intended to minimse visibility of the cladding structure beyond the glass line. The diffusion effect also creates contrast with the dark PV cells so that they to stand out during the day. The modules present three different layouts (Fig. 6.15), namely "low", "medium" and "high" transparency according to the density and number of PV cells. The three module types are positioned on the façade in a pre-determined pattern to represent a "seascape".

During the night, the LEDs project onto the panels from the rear side and the diffusive interlayer helps spread the light.

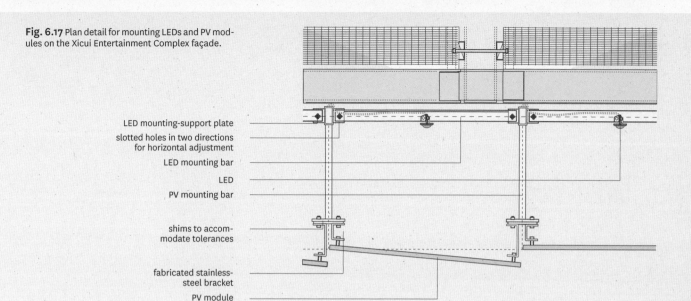

LED mounting-support plate

slotted holes in two directions for horizontal adjustment

LED mounting bar

LED

PV mounting bar

shims to accommodate tolerances

fabricated stainless-steel bracket

PV module

6.6.4 Façade engineering

The rainscreen used for the cladding is a back ventilated type. The wall already incorporates insulation and vapour barriers so installation of the rainscreen was mostly concerned with mounting the PV modules.

The mullions are attached to the horizontal steel trusses and vertical steel columns, which were designed for pre-fabrication in modular units. These units were a convenient size for ease of shipping to the construction site and were structurally connected to the pre-existing building structure. The trusses support catwalks at each level providing easy access for maintenance and cleaning.

Each module is bolt-supported by a four point spider clamp support system, which is connected to the stainless steel mullions (**Fig. 6.17**, **Fig. 6.18**). These spider clamp connections provide slots suitable to receive the fixing bolts from the glass modules. Gaskets around the fixing bolts in the glass accommodate live loads, sliding, rotation out of plane of the modules so that they can expand, contract and flex in response to wind and weather without imposing bending moments through the fixings.

The steel structure supporting the PV modules also supports the grid of LED fixtures set back 600 mm behind the glass surface. After the system installation, each LED fixture was aligned to centre its beam on its PV module.

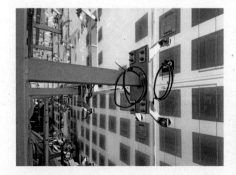

Fig. 6.18 Rear view of the PV array showing cladding fixtures, supporting structure and wiring connections.
Photo: Frank P. Palmer
Courtesy: Simone Giostra & Partners/Arup

Fig. 6.19 Close-up of the laminated-glass PV modules showing how some are tilted 5° out of the plane of the array to increase the variety of sunlight reflections.
Photo: Frank P. Palmer
Courtesy: Simone Giostra & Partners/Arup

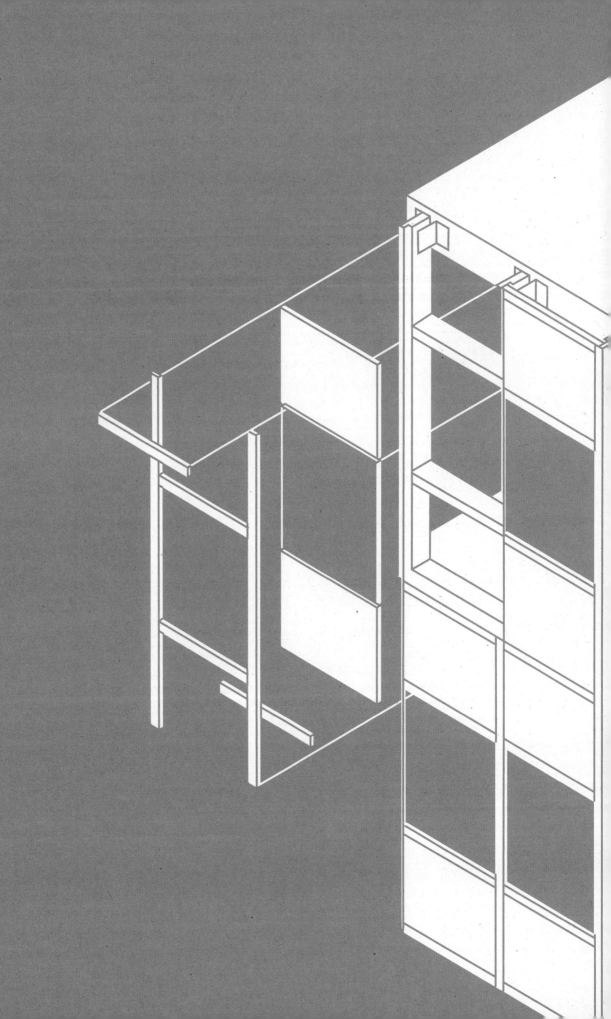

7. STICK-SYSTEM CURTAIN WALLS

7.1 General

Curtain walls can be divided in two main types according to the system of fabrication and installation: stick systems and unitised panels. The traditional curtain-wall construction is the stick system, where mullions and transoms are assembled on site, which is the subject of this chapter. Unitised curtain walls are delivered to site as pre-assembled large panels, fully glazed, for speedy installation. This system is covered in Chapter 8.

The stick system, also known as mullion/transom system, is a fairly common form of curtain-walling construction. The system is delivered to site as individual components, finished, cut and machined. Such components include mullions (vertical members), transoms (horizontal members), vision glazing (for vision window areas), opaque glazed units or insulated pressed metal panels (for non-vision spandrel areas), gaskets and bracketry for securing the cladding system to the building structure.

Stick-system curtain walls are widely used for low-rise buildings where a low-medium size system is required. They are not recommended for high-rise construction because of the need for scaffolding to the outside of the building to allow installation and the limited capability to accommodate live loads.

This form of construction relies heavily on a skilled site workforce since it is assembled on site rather than in a factory. As a result, quality-control procedures need to focus on site operations.

7.2 Principles of construction

With a curtain-walling system, the mullions transfer the horizontal wind forces and vertical gravity loads of the façade to the floors and structural frame of the building (Fig. 7.1). The mullions are usually storey-high, but they can be continuous over two or a maximum of three storeys, subject to available length of extrusions.

Transoms are fitted between the mullions to form frames defining the vision and spandrel areas and to carry the deadload of the infill panels. These are fitted with fixed glazing or opening windows in the vision areas. The spandrel areas are fitted with glass, metal, stone or other opaque materials.

Movement joints are provided in the framework to accommodate movements in the framework itself, differential movements of the framework relative to the building structure and of the building structure.

The outer weather seal between the infill panel and the frame, this being the first line of defence, is formed by gaskets and sometimes sealing tapes or sealants. The infill panels are typically clamped in place with continuous-pressure plates screw-fixed to the framework. Therefore, the typical design implies expressed mullion and transom pressure plates, with or without decorative cover caps. (This means that the mullions and transoms are deliberately emphasised, rather than blending in or being hidden to give an appearance of uniformity.) Special toggle fixing systems allow a flush façade design by omitting the external grid formed by those pressure plates.

Behind the first line of defence is a pressure-equalised cavity. The cavity requires small holes to the external environment to allow ventilation and drainage at the bottom. To deal with the driving force generated by wind pressure, shielded holes are provided through the pressure plate. Whilst the system is designed to minimise the ingress of water into the cavity behind the first line of defence, the cavity should be considered as a wet area. The inner airseal is formed by the inner gasket, which acts as a second line of defence.

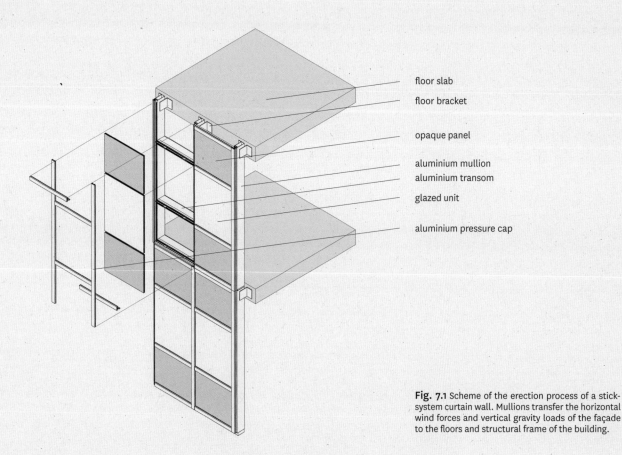

floor slab

floor bracket

opaque panel

aluminium mullion
aluminium transom

glazed unit

aluminium pressure cap

Fig. 7.1 Scheme of the erection process of a stick-system curtain wall. Mullions transfer the horizontal wind forces and vertical gravity loads of the façade to the floors and structural frame of the building.

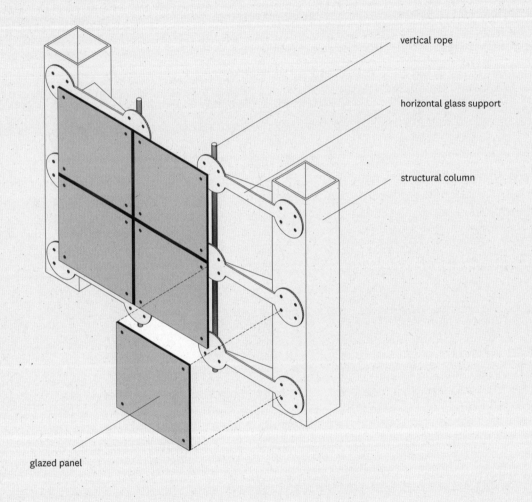

Fig. 7.2 Schematic of secondary structure to support structural bolted glazing

vertical rope

horizontal glass support

structural column

glazed panel

7.3 Glazing systems

This section details a number of different glazing systems. See Chapter 8 for other types of glazing.

7.3.1 Stainless-steel toggles for glazing

An alternative method of fixing a glazing unit to the aluminium frame is to use stainless-steel toggles screwed in to the main aluminium members. These toggles slide into local fixing channels which are integrated into the spacer between the two panes of the double-glazed unit. An additional silicone seal or gasketry closing the gap between adjacent glass panels provides a final weather seal.

Fig. 7.3 Detail of brackets for structural bolted glazing
Photo courtesy: fischerwerke

7.3.2 Structural bolted glazing

Single- or double-glazed units made of toughened glass are assembled with special bolts and brackets and supported by a secondary structure to create a near transparent façade or roof with a flush external surface (**Fig. 7.2**, **Fig. 7.3** and case study 6.6 in Chapter 6).
Toughened glass needs to be used in this case because the glazed panes are drilled and the glass must resist the concentrated loads that apply around the holes.
The joints between adjacent panes/glass units are weathersealed on site with wet-applied sealant.
In renovation projects with thermally insulated façades, this type of façade may be used as an additional exterior glass skin providing a different visual appearance and, where the new outer skin is sealed, a thermal and acoustic buffer zone. The spacing between the two skins varies depending on the cleaning-access strategy. It is either 150–200 mm for "narrow twin skins" requiring all internal panels to be openable, or it is a minimum of 600 mm wide to allow for access walkways between the two skins (see Chapter 9 on double-skin façades). There are several patents of point-fixed system available on the market today, each offering particular characteristics.
Either type of application is suited to integration of PV modules although the concealment of cabling and inverters contradicts the generally "transparent" nature of bolted glazing.

7.3.3 Glazing beads

In masonry walls, glass fixed into frames with glazing beads is the most common form of window construction. The weight of the glass is transferred via supporting blocks. The glazing beads provide the mechanical fixing for the sheets and the sealing.

7.4 Integration of PV modules

PV modules can be integrated into stick-curtain wall systems either in the vision area or in the spandrel area of the façade. Single- or double-glazed units can be replaced by clear or opaque, single- or double-glazed PV modules (**Fig. 7.4**). PV modules can be mounted and weatherproofed into the façade in the same way as ordinary glass panels.

If PV modules are integrated into the vision area of the curtain wall, the modules would be laminated onto a carrier glass that would form the outer lite of a clear double-glazed unit and include low emissivity, solar control or high-performance coatings. To avoid glass breakage due to thermal shock, the glass laminate would be likely to feature heat-treated glazing. The build-up of the double-glazed unit would also need to withstand other loads such as wind loading and impact from building occupants. More details on glazing are given in Chapter 8.

If PV modules are integrated into the spandrel area of the curtain wall, an opaque or semi-transparent solar laminate could be used. The semi-transparent type would be used in a shadow box to create an impression of depth and light penetration, though there is no actual vision through the glass to the building interior. The PV modules could be integrated into single or double-glazed units. If a double glazed unit is chosen, coatings or ceramic fritting can be applied to one of the panes, but care must be taken that the efficiency is not reduced by shading the actual PV modules.

For a spandrel or shadow-box construction, the cavity behind the PV module needs to be drained and pressure-equalised. The inner part is formed by an insulated panel. The heat build-up in the spandrel cavity or shadow box would require heat-treated glass to be used for the outer pane.

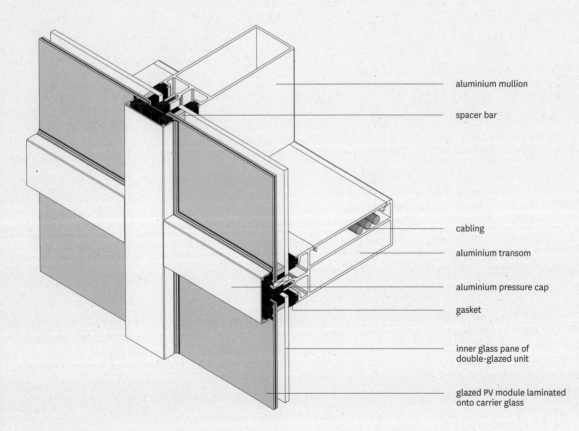

aluminium mullion

spacer bar

cabling

aluminium transom

aluminium pressure cap

gasket

inner glass pane of double-glazed unit

glazed PV module laminated onto carrier glass

Fig. 7.4 Detail of PV modules and connections in a stick system curtain wall. The PV modules are laminated onto a carrier glass.

PV modules could also be built into the spandrel area of a curtain wall by integrating the PV module into the outer face of an insulated sandwich panel. Sandwich panels are typically constructed with two pressed-aluminium sheets suitably spaced apart to house a layer of insulation material. The outer sheet could be replaced by a PV module. The edges are factory-sealed and can be detailed to a thickness matching to double-glazed units so that the panels can be glazed into mullions and transoms without modifications.

Another possibility would be to use hook-on or bolt-on PV modules forward of the spandrel area of the curtain wall after the system is constructed and made weather-tight, thus forming a rainscreen (see Chapter 6). If all conventional elements (such as glazing, insulation, seals) are in place, PV modules could be post-fixed to proprietary bracketry attached to the spandrel area of the cladding system. A drained, ventilated external cavity would space-off the PV module from the insulated panel. The cavity would assure free cooling of the cells to maintain their efficiency.

Issues that require particular attention during design and detailing are:
— the location and integration of the junction box on the PV module
— the routing of electrical wiring along or through mullions and transoms
  (Fig. 7.4)
— the weather- and air-tightness of perforations in the mullion and transom
  extrusions
— the junction box and the wiring exiting at edges of double-glazed units and
  the durability of the edge seals
— the ability of the PV panel to take wind and maintenance loads

A key question is whether to have all wiring externally with only one penetration to the inside or lots of penetrations and the bulk of the wiring internally. Both approaches need careful consideration relating to space requirements, access, weathering performance, etc.

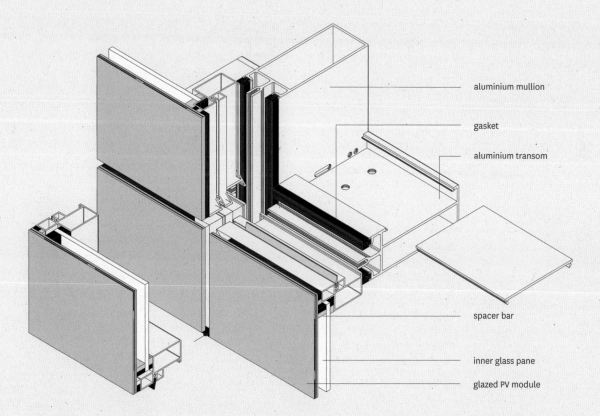

aluminium mullion

gasket

aluminium transom

spacer bar

inner glass pane

glazed PV module

Fig. 7.5 Exploded view of a stick system curtain wall with PV modules fixed with structural silicone.

7.5 Maintenance & replacement

Maintenance and replacement of a stick system curtain wall with integrated PV modules typically occurs from the outside. An important issue to consider when designing the building envelope is the replacement of glazing units and PV modules. Easy access to external and/or internal fixings and wiring is required and needs to be built into the design.

If PV modules are integrated into the cladding system as glazing, replacement would normally comprise dismantling of pressure plates, screws and gaskets to release the infill panels from the framework. Replacement of such units means a temporary/partial removal of the weathering protection of the building envelope.

For low-rise buildings, access from the outside can be provided by means of ladders or possibly a cherry picker. Higher buildings are often equipped with a cleaning cradle running on a track along the perimeter of the roof which can be lowered to gain access to every elevation.

When deciding upon a replacement strategy, the designer needs also to consider the size and weight of the glazing units and PV modules. For larger components, the access strategy and equipment may need to include separate lifting and handling equipment.

7.6 Stick and cassette curtain wall

Stick and cassette curtain walls are a further development of the traditional stick system curtain wall in an attempt to improve quality by increasing pre-fabrication. The external appearance is more of a picture frame aesthetic instead of the grid effect of a stick system curtain wall with pressure caps.

A structural frame of mullions and transoms is constructed on site, as for a traditional stick system. Afterwards, the vision and spandrel areas of the façade are fitted as pre-assembled panels known as cassettes. The cassettes include a glazing unit or an insulation panel mounted onto a secondary carrier frame. All weather seals are factory fitted to the cassette. The cassettes are fixed back to the structural framing using mechanical fixings.

Stick and cassette system curtain walls are an upgrade from traditional stick system façades since they depend less on site assembly of components by a skilled workforce. Primary weather seals can be made in a carefully controlled environment where a quality control system can be put in place. However, the installation of cassettes in to the primary cladding frames remains a vulnerable step in the construction process. Increased manufacturing lead-in times are balanced by reduced site operations.

Fig. 7.6 South façade of the Tobias Grau GmbH Head office west building in Rellingen (D) showing the PV structural glazed panels.
Photo courtesy: Schüco International KG

7.7 Case study: Tobias Grau GmbH Head Office

Location

Town, country: Rellingen, Germany
Latitude, longitude, elevation: 53.631°, 9.885°, 16 m
Average horizontal irradiation: 2.73 kWh/(m²·day)

PV

Area: 179 m²
Peak power specification: 18 kW$_p$
Power output: 10,800 kWh/y
Individual module dimensions: 1970 × 1430 mm
Technology: polycrystalline silicon
Manufacturer: Schüco

Building

Type: office
Height, storeys: 10 m, 2
Floor area: 4160 m²
Architects: BRT Architects
Completed: 2001

7.7.1 Background

The lighting company, Tobias Grau GmbH, required functional spaces in an attractive shape with innovative technologies for their new offices in Rellingen near Hamburg. The design of the architect, Bothe Richter Teherani, responded with an elongated, oval unit (Fig. 7.7) repeated for the two buildings. The two pipe-shaped buildings are parallel to each other and connected by a perpendicular extension, giving an H-shape to the complex.

The main structure is created by laminated-timber arches spanning 20 m and installed 5 m one to each other. Aluminium sandwich panels are attached to the timber structures and create the tube shape of the buildings. This is closed towards the North with a fully glazed, unshaded, inward-sloped façade and towards the South with a PV façade. The east and west elevations present curved glazed façades which are protected from the solar radiation by external, movable louvres, spanning 2.5 m each.

Because of the limited height of the façades (about 8 m) and because of the desired flush appearance, the modules have been installed on a stick-curtain walling system with structural silicone glazing.

Fig. 7.7 View from southeast onto the pipe-shape of
the Tobias Grau building showing the south and east
façades.
Photo courtesy: Schüco International KG

Fig. 7.8 View of the south façade from inside showing the spacing between the PV cells letting in filtered natural daylight.
Photo courtesy: Tobias Grau GmbH

7.7.2 PV integration

The vertical south façades of the two buildings together present an overall area of 179 m² for PV integration. The west building **(Fig. 7.8)** has an area of 128 m² for 45 modules.

The modules are clear laminates with blue polycrystalline cells. The cells have a 10 mm spacing so that the modules let some natural daylight through the façade with the cells acting as solar shading device. This aspect together with the high transparency of the other façades makes the daylight one of the key aspects of this project. Module dimensions are 1.97 × 1.43 m.

The two PV systems were funded by the government of Schleswig-Holstein and have a specification of 18 kW$_P$. They generate about 11 MWh per year.

8. UNITISED CURTAIN WALLS

8.1 General

Unitised curtain walling was developed to overcome the problems associated with the installation of stick systems (see Chapter 7) and to reduce the on-site installation time. It consists of large panels, usually as big as can be transported from the factory to site. Typically, unitised panels are storey height and 1.5 m wide. In their most developed form these panels can be storey height and up to 9 m long.

As manufactured in the factory, the panels contain all the necessary elements that the external building fabric would require: external weathering elements, insulation, vapour barrier, structural framing, fire protection, vision panels and internal finish. This type of panel can be considered as a basic building block or unit of construction and is referred to as a unitised panel.

The external weathering element is frequently made of metal or natural stone in the non-vision areas and of double-glazed units in the vision areas. One design variant to create depth or light effects in the spandrel zone is a shadow-box construction where the spandrel area is made up of a single- or double-glazed unit, an air cavity and an insulated panel on the inside

Installation of unitised systems on the building is relatively simple and can be carried out from the floor slabs inside the building, therefore eliminating the need for external scaffolding (**Fig. 8.1, Fig. 8.2**). Since most of the work is factory-based, the complete operation can be organised, carried out and supervised much more effectively and efficiently than the work required for a site-assembled system, as is required for the stick system.

Unitised systems are particularly suited to highly articulated façades providing visual interest which are often finished in heavy materials, for example natural stone. They therefore tend to be used on the more prestigious city-centre commercial developments where the cladding would be of bespoke nature and therefore in the middle to high cost range.

Fig. 8.1 Erection of a unitised curtain-wall system (without PV).
Photo: Nicolò Guariento

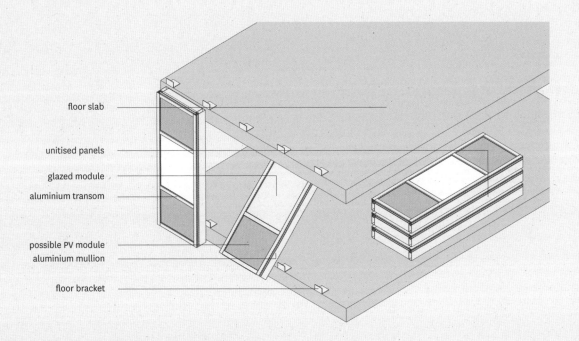

floor slab

unitised panels

glazed module

aluminium transom

possible PV module
aluminium mullion

floor bracket

Fig. 8.2 Schematic of unitised curtain-wall storage on site and the erection process from inside without the need for external scaffolding.

8.2 Structural frame

The structural frame of the panel is designed to carry the full weight of the panel plus all superimposed loads, primarily the wind load. Typically, extruded aluminium mullions and transoms are assembled to form a rigid frame. Pre-formed EPDM or silicone gaskets are slid into gasket races in the extrusions. Afterwards, a double-glazed unit is mounted in the glazing rebate and fixed by means of pressure caps or structural silicone (Fig. 8.3).

The construction is pressure-equalised (see Chapter 6). The external face forms the primary weather barrier. In the case of stone facing this would be formed with either open joints, or sealed joints with provision for drainage and ventilation between layers. The inner airtight seal is formed by the airseal/vapour barrier in the panel and in the panel-to-panel joints using preformed gaskets.

The material used for the external facing is a major factor in deciding the material to be used in the frame. Natural-stone facing, typically 40–50 mm thick, might require a steel or reinforced aluminium frame due to its weight. A lightweight metal facing may only require a frame made out of simple aluminium extrusions. Fire-resistance requirements will also dictate frame material type. The facing is fixed to the frame using studs, bolts or rails, with allowance for a cavity of approximately 50 mm in addition to rigid insulation and a vapour barrier. Fire lining boards and internal finishes are applied to the internal face of the frame.

Unitised systems are gravity loaded at each floor level and usually accommodate live load deflections not greater than 10 mm to 12 mm.

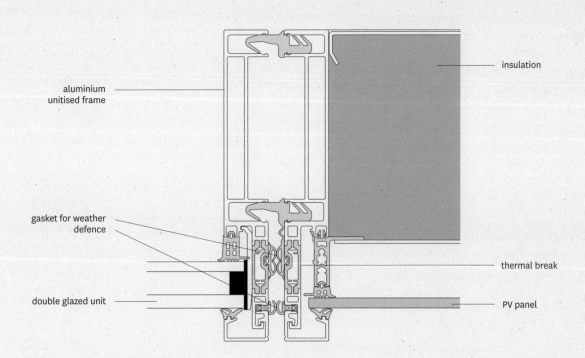

aluminium unitised frame

insulation

gasket for weather defence

thermal break

double glazed unit

PV panel

Fig. 8.3 Horizontal section through a unit stack joint showing the tolerance space for differential movements.

8.3 Other glazing systems

The following glazing systems are used in the construction of unitised curtain walls. For other types of glazing, see Chapter 7.

8.3.1 Dry glazing

When the system is dry glazed, the pressure caps hold the glass in place by means of wedge gaskets, which should have moulded corners to form a continuous weather seal. This glazing system implies exposed split mullion and transom profiles.
In the case of dry glazing for a stick system (see Chapter 7), this system is also called mechanical fixing with pressure plate. Units are typically sealed with gaskets and retained with a pressure plate, screw-fixed every 150–300 mm. The pressure plate is generally hidden with a snap-on cover cap, which can be removed in order to access the screw fixings. Fixings must be secured to the correct torque to retain the glazing/infill panels and to ensure proper compression of the gasket for weather sealing.

8.3.2 Wet glazing

When the system is wet glazed, the glass is bonded to the aluminium frame with structural silicone. Structural silicone glazing allows a flush design of the glazing, eliminating the need for exposed profiles along the framing members. For durability reasons, the structural silicone bond should be applied under controlled factory conditions.
From an aesthetic point of view, this system of glazing offers a flush appearance and for this reason is usually appreciated by the architects. The risk with this system is that when a panel needs replacing (for example because it is broken), the silicone seal needs to be cut and a new seal made on site which requires stringent quality control to achieve a durable and reliable bond.
Some exceptional situations, such as extremely cold or hot climates or for bomb-blast requirements or due to local planners' regulation, local mechanical restraint clips are required. These provide an additional fixing mechanism in case the structural silicone bond breaks.

8.3.3 Hybrid glazing

To avoid having to apply a structural silicone seal on site, a hybrid system is often used where the glass is silicone bonded to an aluminium sub-frame. The sub-frame can in turn be dry fixed to the main structural cladding frame with gasket seals.
If a panel needs replacement, the mechanical fixings are unlocked to release the aluminium carrier frame. A new panel is then sealed in the sub-frame with structural silicone in factory conditions. The replacement panel is brought to site and again mounted into position without the need for site-applied sealant.

8.4 Integration of PV modules

PV modules can be integrated into unitised curtain wall systems either in the vision area or in the spandrel area of the façade. Single or double-glazed units can be replaced by clear or opaque, single- or double-glazed PV modules (Fig. 8.4). PV modules can be mounted and weather-proofed into the façade in the same way as ordinary glass panels. The PV modules can be integrated into the pre-fabricated panels during their assembly in the factory. All penetrations of the electrical wiring through the aluminium framing members or weather seals can therefore be sealed in factory conditions with a close control on quality.

To maintain this degree of quality control, conventional systems with four-side structural silicone seals are not recommended due to the need for site application of structural silicone in case of replacement.

If PV modules are integrated into the vision area of the curtain wall, the modules form the outer lite of a clear double-glazed unit, with low emissivity, solar control or high-performance coatings added. To avoid glass breakage due to thermal shock, the glass laminate would likely comprise heat-treated glazing. Integration is generally as for stick-system curtain wall (see Chapter 7).

Care is needed with silicone jointing with PV modules. As with laminated safety glass, care should be taken that the silicone within the outer weathering seals cannot come into contact and react with the acrylic spacers of glass-glass modules or with laminate films (EVA/PVB). To avoid contact, silicone profiles must be inserted into the joints and used as spacers.

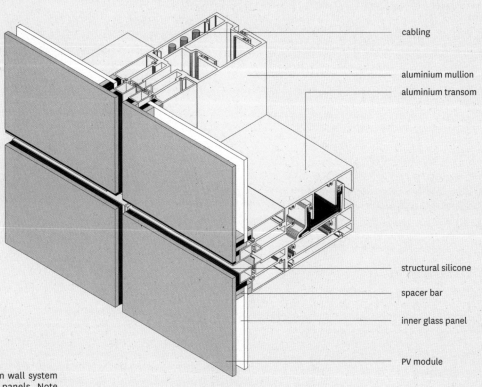

cabling

aluminium mullion

aluminium transom

structural silicone

spacer bar

inner glass panel

PV module

Fig. 8.4 Detail of a unitised curtain wall system with PV modules in double-glazed panels. Note routing of cables through the mullion.

→ 8.4

When using insulating glass modules, even more care should be taken with the joints as the cabling along the glass edges must be routed out of the modules and through the joints into the supporting construction. The cable insulation should not come into direct contact with the silicone.

In pressure-plate system of glazing, the mullion cap depth must be kept to a minimum to avoid adverse shadowing on PV cells. Alternatively, flush application of a structural silicone seal between PV glazing units eliminates shadowing effects but increases weather seal and durability problems for PV panel edges.

8.5 Maintenance and replacement

Maintenance and replacement of a unitised curtain wall with integrated PV modules would often occur from the outside. Important issues to consider when designing the building envelope are the replacement of glazing units and PV modules.

Easy access to external and/or internal fixings and wiring needs to be carefully considered from the onset of the design.

Replacement of damaged infill units would normally comprise demounting of gaskets, screws, pressure plates and/or mechanical fixings to release the infill panels from the unitised framework and installation of the replacement panels.

Replacement of such units means a temporary/partial removal of the weathering protection of the building envelope.

Hook-on or bolt-on PV modules allow easy replacement without the need to break the existing weathering protection system.

If the system is equipped with sub-frames which hold the infill panels, all primary weather seals of replacement carrier frames can be made in a controlled environment; this remains an advantage of a stick and cassette system.

Unitised curtain walling is mostly employed on multi-storey buildings often equipped with a cleaning cradle running on a track along the perimeter of the roof that can be lowered along guides to gain access to every elevation.

When deciding on a replacement strategy, the designer needs also to consider the size and weight of the glazing units and PV modules. Access strategy and equipment should allow easy handling of larger components.

8.6 Case study: Alan Gilbert Building

Location

Town, country: Melbourne, Australia
Latitude, longitude, elevation: −37.800°, 144.959°, 52 m
Average horizontal irradiation: 4.12 kWh/(m²·day)

PV

Area: 426 m²
Peak power specification: 46 kW$_P$
Power output: 40,000 kWh/y
Individual module dimensions:
1220 × 939 mm to 2664 × 1895 mm
Technology: polycrystalline silicon
Manufacturer: BP Solar

Building

Type: Faculty of Economics and Commerce
Height, storeys: 24 m estimate, 8
Floor area: 4550 m² estimate
Architects: Metier3
Completed: 2001

8.6.1 Background

The Alan Gilbert Building represents the first large-scale building-integrated PV project new-build in Australia (Fig. 8.5). Completed in December 2001, the eight-storey building is part of Melbourne's new University Square Campus.
The top-level of the building hosts the building services and covers an overall area of 426 m². It presents an inclined façade. The façade is unitised because it is high-rise (above 3 stories) and inclined inwards, so assembly from within is easier.

Fig. 8.5 External view of the Alan Gilbert Building
showing the PV in the two top storeys only.
Photo: Dianna Snape
Courtesy: Arup

Fig. 8.6 Close-up of the north façade of the Alan Gilbert Building showing the contrast in appearance between the polycrystalline PV modules and the conventional façade beneath. Pressure plates which line up with the internal primary structure of slabs and columns are clearly visible.
Photo: Dianna Snape
Courtesy: Arup

Fig. 8.7 View onto the east end of the Alan Gilbert Building showing the 70° to 74° tilt from horizontal of the top two levels of the north façade.
Photo: John Gollings
Courtesy: Arup

8.6.2 PV integration

Glass-to-glass laminated polycrystalline cells are spaced in order to allow part of the incident daylight to pass through the façade (Fig. 8.8). In particular the outer layer is a low-iron heat-strengthened glass panel 6 mm thick, whereas the inner is a clear heat-strengthened glass panel 6 mm thick. The two panes are separated by 2 mm of liquid (resin) interlayer, within which the polycrystalline cells are embedded. The choice of polycrystalline cells is related to the lower cost in comparison with monocrystalline cells and to aesthetic aspects since they match the appearance of the rest of the building.

The 21,400 polycrystalline cells were produced in Sydney by BP Solar and sent to Flabeg in Germany, where they were laminated to the carrier glass. After the lamination process the panels were sent back to Australia where Permasteelisa created the unitised framed modules to be directly installed on site. The modules were installed with structural silicone glazing. Every fifth module is externally framed with a pressure plate, which creates a pattern on the façade reflecting the internal primary structure of slabs and columns (Fig. 8.6).

The PV façade is made of 148 modules with eight different sizes (ranging from 1220 × 939 mm to 2664 × 1895 mm), each with a different number of cells and thus a different output voltage. The modules are connected together in different groups, which present different output voltages too (Fig. 8.9). For this reason each group has its own inverter, which is designed to receive the specific output from the relevant group of modules.

The installation produces 47.3 kW$_P$ and the generated power feeds the building's services and if the generated electricity exceeds the requirement, the power is exported to the grid network.

Fig. 8.8 Internal view of the "service top floor" showing the appearance of the PV cells from inside and shadows cast on the floor.
Photo: John Gollings
Courtesy: Arup

Fig. 8.9 Connection unit for the PV array in the Alan Gilbert Building showing the semi-transparent façade in the background.
Photo: John Gollings
Courtesy: Arup

8.7 Case study: Wal-Mart Experimental Supercenter

Location

Town, country: McKinney, USA
Latitude, longitude, elevation: 33.221°, −96.630°, 197 m
Average horizontal irradiation: 4.54 kWh/(m²·day)

PV

Area: polycrystalline silicon 287 m², thin-film silicon 27 m²
Peak power specification: polycrystalline silicon 32 kW$_P$,
thin-film silicon 3 kW$_P$
Power output: polycrystalline silicon 23,500 kWh/y estimate,
thin-film silicon 2400 kWh/y estimate
Individual module dimensions: 1500×1500 mm
Technology: polycrystalline silicon & thin-film silicon
Manufacturer: Schott Solar

Building

Type: retail
Height, storeys: 11 m estimate, 1
Floor area: 20,000 m²
Architects: LPA Inc.
Completed: 2005

8.7.1 Background

In 2005 Wal-Mart, the largest retailer in the world, opened two experimental stores, one in McKinney, Texas (Fig. 8.10), the other in Aurora, Colorado. The experimental stores were built to evaluate the use of recycled materials, energy-saving technologies and renewable energy.

Between 2005 and 2008, independent laboratories monitored the performance of the installed technologies to measure the potential benefits of implementing sustainable practices into Wal-Mart stores across the USA. Renewable-energy technologies under evaluation included numerous PV arrays, two small wind turbines and a bio-fuel boiler to recycle and burn recovered oil from store operations. Since this was a benchmarking project, Wal-Mart wanted to experiment with as many types of PV materials as possible to see which one was performing best. For this reason the complex uses polycrystalline cells and thin-film amorphous silicon PV, installed on a vertical façade and on the inclined roof.

Fig. 8.10 General view of the Wal-Mart Experimental Supercenter in McKinney (USA).
Photo: Chris Costea
Courtesy: Arup

8.7.2 PV technology in curtain walling

The south-facing façade was an opportunity to use both polycrystalline and thin-film amorphous silicon technologies integrated in horizontal bands on a vertical unitised curtain walling, which runs the whole length of the store (Fig. 8.11). This installation consisted of an upper opaque band made of square polycrystalline cells and a bottom semitransparent band with thin-film amorphous modules. Together they allow natural light to pass through the façade and reach the entrance and the checkout area of the store.

The upper band is made up of 121 laminates of polycrystalline silicon creating a signature "blue stripe" (Fig. 8.11). The lower band has 39 laminates of thin-film silicon with a high degree of transparency. The crystalline modules have a specification of $110\,W_P/m^2$ in contrast to $45\,W_P/m^2$ for the thin-film modules. Together the two types of technology have a total specification of $35\,kW_P$ and estimated output of 26,000 kWh/y.

The modules were manufactured by Schott Solar and factory-assembled by Wausau Window and Wall Systems on frames to meet the aesthetic, structural and weather-tightness requirements. Since the modules were pre-assembled, the installation on site occurred easily and quickly. The frames were set up to accept the wires with male and female leads for easy connection on site. DC current is inverted to AC current and wired directly to the power grid.

8.7.3 PV technology in roofing

The store also has building integrated PV in various roofs.

The Garden Center canopy has polycrystalline silicon modules inclined for optimum output (Fig. 8.12). There are 44 laminates with a total specification of $11\,kW_P$ and predicted output of 14,600 kWh/y.

90 laminates of thin-film amorphous silicon thin-film amorphous silicon modules are integrated into the horizontal roofs of the vestibules (Fig. 8.13). These have an area of $78\,m^2$, specification of $6.75\,kW_P$ and predicted output of 8400 kWh/y.

A third PV technology consists of thin-film silicon laminates adhered directly to the roof membrane and used on the roof of the Tire and Lube Express. The laminate assemblies are manufactured by United Solar Systems of Troy, Michigan, and adhered to roofing membrane material by Solar Integrated Technologies. There are three laminate assemblies with an area of $53\,m^2$, specification of $4.6\,kW_P$ and predicted output of 5700 kWh/y.

In total the two stores has $57\,kW_P$ and an estimated output of 54,600 kWh/y.

Fig. 8.11 Internal view of the checkout area of the Wal-Mart Experimental Supercenter showing the "blue stripe" of polycrystalline modules along the top of the façade. The clearer part of the façade is semitransparent thin-film amorphous PV modules.
Photo: Chris Costea
Courtesy: Arup

Fig. 8.12 Interior view of the garden center showing the polycrystalline PV modules in the inclined roof on the South side.
Photo: Chris Costea
Courtesy: Arup

Fig. 8.13 Interior of one of the vestibules showing thin-film amorphous modules in the horizontal roof.
Photo: Chris Costea
Courtesy: Arup

8. UNITISED CURTAIN WALLS

9. DOUBLE-SKIN FAÇADES

9.1 General

The double-skin façade is a system that consists of two building skins separated by a ventilated cavity (Fig. 9.1). The main aim of the cavity is to vary the physical properties of the façade throughout the year, improving the building's performance. Between the heat-insulated inner façade and the outer skin is an unheated thermal buffer zone, which is ventilated if required and can incorporate movable solar shading devices. Double-skin façades are designed to adapt to ambient conditions and balance out seasonal climate fluctuations. Thus heat, coldness, light and wind are regulated to attain optimum comfort without any complex technology or use of energy. Sometimes the heat energy that builds up in the cavity is used not just passively but also actively. The outer façade is extremely suitable for integrating photovoltaics since it consists of single glazing and the modules can also provide solar shading.

Most often, a shading device (fixed opaque louvres, fixed or retractable blinds, roller blinds, etc.) is placed within the cavity in order to protect the building from excessive solar radiation or glare. When the cavity is ventilated, the heat resulting from the radiation absorbed at the shading device can be extracted though ventilation means, reducing the secondary solar transmission that enters the building (Fig. 9.2). The effectiveness of shading devices also depends on the properties of their surface (colour, finish).

This system can provide an adequate control of the internal environmental conditions both from the solar point of view (in the case of movable blinds) by operating on the angle and position of the shading device, and from the thermal point of view by controlling the ventilation within the cavity.

From an aesthetic point of view, a double-skin façade allows the concept of a clean, highly glazed façade, since the internal skin can be used as effective thermal envelope. Thanks to a second glass skin, building users can also leave windows open during various climatic conditions such as wind, rain, etc. The first or exterior part of the skin shields the entire building, and by doing so, permits natural ventilation through air corridors between the skins. Windows can be left open 24 hours a day and not compromise interior comfort.

With a double-skin façade it is possible to achieve the same excellent acoustic insulation with the windows open as with that obtained in classical glass façades with the windows closed.

In wintertime, the air stored between the glass skins is heated by the solar gain, thus improving both the heat-insulating functions of the façade and its thermal performance, as well as reducing heating costs.

With natural ventilation, so-called night cooling can significantly reduce the costs of air-conditioning in the summer.

Fig. 9.1 Example of a double-skin façade (without PV integration).
Photo: Chris Gascoigne
Courtesy: VIEW

9.2 Principles of construction

The behaviour of a double-skin façade is mainly determined by the ventilation within the cavity and the means by which the air movement is driven.

The ventilation strategies described below are mostly used in central Europe and regions with similar climate. Different strategies are chosen according to the different weather conditions.

9.2.1 Natural ventilation

In a naturally ventilated façade, the air movement relies on pressure difference without the aid of motorised elements. The pressure difference is caused by the wind and by the stack effect (or chimney effect) driven by thermal buoyancy inside the cavity: cold air enters the cavity from a lower level, runs upwards while it is heated and is released on an upper level. This kind of ventilation is totally dependent on the boundary conditions of the system (internal and external temperatures, wind pressure) and its control by the building management system is limited to the control of dampers inserted in the openings through the two skins.

If the stack effect does not guarantee the required level of ventilation, the system can be equipped with fans, which are switched on only during the periods with insufficient natural ventilation. In this case we have a fan-supported ventilated façade.

In a typical central-European climate, a naturally ventilated façade in summer would have an external air intake and an outward outtake (externally ventilated) which provide a cooling effect on the shading devices (Fig. 9.2); in winter the dampers are closed and the cavity is used as a buffer zone, reducing the thermal transmittance of the façade and thus the thermal losses from the building (Fig. 9.3).

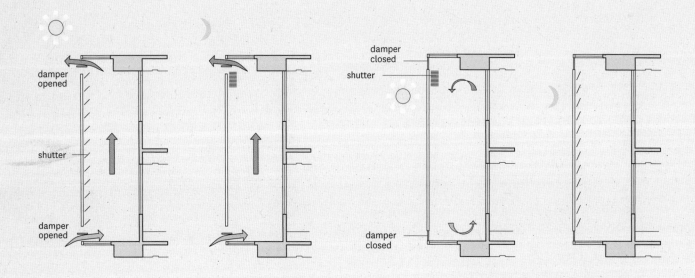

Fig. 9.2 Summer operation of a naturally ventilated façade showing airflow through the façade space: (left) during the day when the shutter is down to reflect direct radiation; (right) during the night when the shutter is pulled up.

Fig. 9.3 Winter operation of a naturally ventilated façade with damper for external air closed. It shows the façade space: (left) during the day when the shutter is pulled up allowing direct radiation in; (right) during the night when the shutter is down to minimise radiative losses from inside.

9. DOUBLE-SKIN FAÇADES

9.2.2 Mechanically ventilated

In mechanical ventilation, the air that passes within the two skins is then sent to the air-handling unit (AHU). In a typical central-European climate during summer the air usually enters the cavity from outside, runs within the façade, into the air-handling system and it is then released outside. In winter the air enters the cavity from outside, it is pre-heated while running along the façade and heated in the air-handling unit and released in the internal environment (Fig. 9.4).

9.2.3 Hybrid ventilation

In hybrid ventilation, both natural and mechanical ventilation strategies are used. In particular, in a typical centra-European climate, the façade is naturally externally (or fan-supported) ventilated during summer (which guarantees a cooling effect on the shading devices), whereas it is mechanically ventilated during winter (Fig. 9.5).

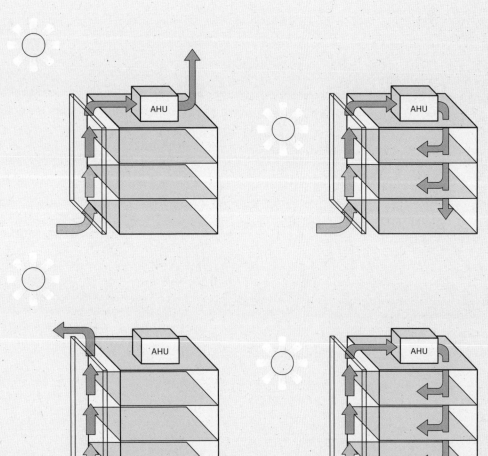

Fig. 9.4 Mechanically ventilated façade showing operation: (left) in summer; (right) in winter. (AHU=Air-handling unit)

Fig. 9.5 Hybrid ventilated façade showing operation: (left) in summer; (right) in winter. (AHU=Air handling unit)

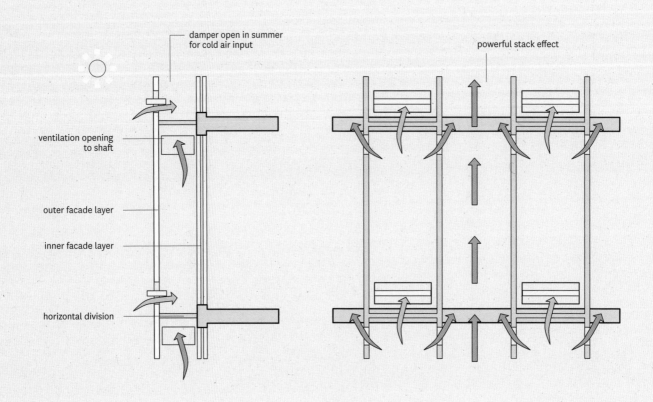

Fig. 9.6 A shaft box ventilated façade: (left) in section; (right) view on the front.

9.2.4 Ventilation paths

An important factor influencing the performance and the ventilation type of a double-skin façade is the path the air is forced to follow within the cavity and the way in which the cavity itself is subdivided.

The cavity might need to be divided horizontally and vertically to correspond with the framing of PV modules, for instance. If this restricts the dimensions of the cavity, this might prevent the stack effect, meaning that a natural-ventilation strategy will not be feasible.

Where the cavity is divided into deep, horizontal compartments, this creates a corridor for people to walk in. If the cavity is one storey high and can extend across a whole floor, it will have a limited stack effect. This configuration will not be ideal for natural ventilation.

In order to encourage the use of natural ventilation, the cavity can be horizontally and vertically subdivided so that the façade is made of an alternation of juxtaposed modules. With this option the air accesses to the cavity from the bottom of a module and, before getting out of the cavity, is brought along different modules by passing through vertical ventilation ducts (Fig. 9.6). This will increase the stack effect and promote the use of natural ventilation on double-skin façades.

Fig. 9.7 Multi-storey double-skin façade with only a horizontal grid separating floor levels.
Photo: Harris Poirazis

9.2.5 Multi-storey

Another case in which the double-skin façade is generally naturally ventilated is the so-called multi-storey double-skin façade (Fig. 9.7). This type of façade presents a big cavity which is not subdivided either horizontally or vertically. Only a horizontal grid divides the floor levels in order to access the cavity from the inside of the building.

Similar to the multi-storey double-skin façade above described is the multi-storey louvres façade. In this case the outer skin is composed of pivoting louvres which are not airtight even in the closed position.

9.2.6 Performance of each skin

One important aspect of double-skin façades is the performance of the two glazing systems. In general one of the two skins is highly performing from the thermal point of view (usually a double-glazed unit with low-emissivity coated glass) and provides a significant thermal separation between the cold external environment and the warm internal room. The other skin is usually less performing and its aim is to create the cavity between the two skins.

The position of the high-performance skin depends on the intake/outtake strategy, which can affect the condensation risk. Generally it should be considered that if the internal air gets in contact with the cold outer skin, it needs to be highly performing in order to reduce the risk of condensation. In the particular case of PV integration on the external skin, the condensation risk may be reduced by the heating effect of the PV panels.

9.3 Integration of PV modules

In order to obtain the highest performance from the PV modules, they need to be installed on the external skin, which is usually made of fully glazed panels.
In general a double-skin façade is built by installing double-skin unitised modules, but the two skins can also be installed separately using either a stick system or a unitised system. For this reason the integration of PV modules on a double-skin façade occurs exactly as described in the previous chapters, by replacing the single- or double-glazed units of the external skin with single- or double-glazed PV modules.

Since PV modules are usually integrated into the vision area of the curtain wall, the module would form the outer lite of a clear double glazed unit, equipped with low emissivity, solar control or high-performance coatings. To avoid glass breakage due to thermal shock, the glass laminate would likely comprise heat-treated glazing. The build-up of the double-glazed unit would also need to withstand structural actions such as wind loading and meet safety requirements with regard to impact from building occupants.

If the external skin presents a spandrel area, an opaque or semitransparent solar laminate could be used. The PV module could be integrated as a single- or double-glazed unit. If a double-glazed unit is chosen, coatings or ceramic fritting can be applied to one of the panes. The cavity behind the PV module would be drained and pressure equalised, and fitted with an insulated sandwich panel finished off with an air and vapour seal.

PV modules can be integrated within the cavity of a double-skin façade system; beyond their main function of electrical-energy producers, they could also protect the internal environment from the excess of solar radiation entering the building through the façade. As an interstitial shading device, PV modules will intercept the incident solar radiation and heat-up, lowering their efficiency. For this reason, the air within the cavity of the double-skin façade can be used as cooling device for the PV modules.

9.4 Maintenance and replacement

An important issue to consider when designing the building envelope is the replacement of glazing and PV modules. Easy access to external and/or internal fixings and wiring needs to be carefully considered from the outset of the design.

For PV modules integrated into the outer skin of a double-skin façade, maintenance and replacement of the outer skin would often occur from the outside in the same way as a unitised panel (see Chapter 7). Replacement of damaged infill units would normally comprise demounting of gaskets, screws, pressure plates and/or mechanical or toggle fixings. These release the infill panels from the unitised framework and allow installation of the replacement panels. Note that replacement of such units entails a temporary and partial removal of the weathering protection of the building envelope.

Hook-on or bolt-on PV modules allow easy replacement without the need to break the existing weathering protection system.
If the system is equipped with sub-frames which hold the infill panels, all primary weather seals of the replacement carrier frames can be made in a controlled environment. This is a distinct advantage of the cassette in a stick and cassette system.
Multi-storey buildings with double-skin façades are often equipped with a cleaning cradle running on a track along the perimeter of the roof. This can be lowered along guides providing access to every elevation.

When deciding on a replacement strategy, the designer needs also to consider the size and weight of the glazing units and PV modules. Access strategy and equipment should allow easy handling of larger components.

For PV modules integrated into the inner skin of a double-skin façade, maintenance and replacement of the inner skin occurs from inside. Access to the buffer zone facilitates the demounting of gasket, screws and/or mechanical or toggle fixings to release the infill panels from the framework.

9.5 Case study:
Pompeu Fabra Library

Location

Town, country: Mataró, Spain
Latitude, longitude, elevation: 41.538°, 2.434°, 37 m
Average horizontal irradiation: 4.31 kWh/(m²·day)

PV

Area: 255 m²
Peak power specification: 20 kW$_P$
Power output: 20,000 kWh/y
Individual module dimensions: 1100 × 2150 mm
Technology: polycrystalline silicon
Manufacturer: ASE, TFM
(Teulades i Façanes Multifunctionals)

Building

Type: public library
Height, storeys: 11 m, 3
Floor area: 1600 m²
Architects: Miquel Brullet i Tenas,
Teulades i Façanes Multifuncionals
Completed: 1996

9.5.1 Background

In the mid-nineties the city of Mataró, 20 km north of Barcelona in Spain, developed a policy instrument for sustainability in order to join the Aalborg Charter (Charter of European cities for sustainability). Within this programme, a strategic line was dedicated to energy end environmental action plans, in which the Pompeu Fabra Library was included.

The Pompeu Fabra Library in Mataró represented one of the first cases of completely integrated PV systems into building, energetic and architectural design. In addition to the energetic and environmental issues, the design of a public library focused the attention on the quality of the light and the external appearance. The challenge of the project was to find the optimum balance between energy strategy, comfort, quality of the interior lighting, aesthetics and economic aspects.

Another aim of the project was to demonstrate the capabilities and skills offered by the European photovoltaic industry. For this reason, various European manufacturers cooperated on this project using different technologies: opaque and semi-transparent monocrystalline, polycrystalline and thin-film amorphous silicon cells. The Pompeu Fabra Library is a simple rectangular building in form. PV arrays were integrated in two parts: the large south side is a double-skin façade and uses semi-transparent PV modules; the roof skylights have monocrystalline and amorphous silicon modules.

The project was subsidised by the Joule II programme of the European Commission's Directorate-General for Science, Research and Development (DG XII).

Fig. 9.8 View from the south of the PV double-skin
façade of the Pompeu Fabra Library, Mataró (E).
Photo: Jordi Miralles

9.5.2 PV integration

The south façade is 39.6 m wide and 6.5 m high, giving a total area of 255 m² for PV integration (**Fig. 9.8**). The façade design is a double-skin ventilated façade with semi-transparent PV modules integrated in the external skin (**Fig. 9.11**). Each module is 1.1 × 2.15 m with polycrystalline cells laminated between two glass panes. The glass is toughened to resist high temperatures and avoid problems of thermal stress. The cells are squared and horizontally spaced of 14 mm which allows daylight to penetrate the building and thus reduce the use of artificial light (**Fig. 9.10**). The PV modules on the façade are grouped in three fields for a total specification of 20 kWₚ. Each field is connected to a separate inverter with these specially selected for their efficiency, harmonic distortion and reliability.

9.5.3 Façade performance

A 150 mm cavity divides the two glazed skins in the double-skin façade to allow mechanical/natural (hybrid) ventilation within the façade (**Fig. 9.9**). In summer the façade is naturally ventilated with the incoming air from outside used to cool the PV cells before it is released in the external environment. In winter the air heated by the PV modules in the cavity is mechanically moved to a heat-recovery system where it is used to warm the fresh-air intake. In this way the ventilation of the curtain wall generates heat and improves the performance of the PV cells at the same time.

A seven-month post-monitoring strategy developed by the University of Barcelona and the Zentrum für Sonnenenergie- und Wasserstoff-Forschung of Stuttgart showed that the overall PV/thermal system performance had an efficiency of 62%.

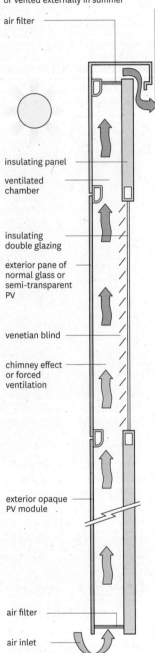

warm air outlet to heating plant in winter or vented externally in summer

air filter

insulating panel

ventilated chamber

insulating double glazing

exterior pane of normal glass or semi-transparent PV

venetian blind

chimney effect or forced ventilation

exterior opaque PV module

air filter

air inlet

Fig. 9.9 Ventilation scheme of the double-skin façade.

Fig. 9.10 Interior view of the PV façade of Pompeu Fabra Library, Mataró, showing how the semi-transparent PV contrasts with the clear glazing of the entrance doors.
Photo: Jordi Miralles

Fig. 9.11 Interior detail of the double-skin façade, showing the semitransparent PV modules in the exterior skin and the wiring connections in the ventilated cavity.
Photo: Jordi Miralles

10. ATRIA AND CANOPIES

10.1 General

Glazed roofs have been a characteristic of modern architecture since the mid-19th century. The quest for light attains the maximum expression when the sky can be made part of the inside building (**Fig. 10.1**). Of course, the risks in this case are not small: we can lose control of light transmission, accelerate heat loss in winter and heat gain in summer, and potentially suffer from roof leaks.

The control of the inner-space conditions remains the more important driver when designing atria or skylights, and PV modules can play an important role, acting as sun-shading elements.

Canopies are similar to atria consisting of horizontal or gently inclined faces, high on a building. They can provide good opportunities for PV integration. See also Chapter 5 for aspects common with shading devices.

Fig. 10.1 Glazed roof of the Central Station in Berlin (D) showing one area of 10×6 panels of PV modules. Photo: Ed Heine

10.2 Principles of construction

The construction of glazed skylights can be based on both stick curtain wall system (see Chapter 7) and unitised curtain wall system (see Chapter 8). The mullions acting as rafters and the transoms acting as counter battens transfer the vertical loads (dead load, wind, snow, maintenance) to the main structure. The mullion dimension is usually not greater than 4m to avoid extra deflection, and they can sometimes be reinforced. The glass infill is a double-glazed unit, with the inner lite laminated to prevent fall-downs.

Important issues of skylight construction, especially when the slope is small, are the risk of condensation in the lower side of the glass and the accumulation of dirt on the upper side of the glass.

On the lower side, the degree of condensation risk must be calculated with appropriate attention to inner ventilation and the use of high-performance coatings, in order to keep the inner face of the glass warm. On the upper side, the degree to which dirt accumulates can be reduced by increasing the slope and by using flush connections between the glass elements, so that rainwater can go flow without interruptions. It is common to use a screw snap-on cover for the sloped mullions and seal with silicone. For the horizontal joints above the transoms, a backer rod is used.

The other relevant issue for skylight construction is the weather-tightness. The mullion-transom structure must be designed so that water penetrating the joints between the glass units can be controlled and transferred via the transoms and then the mullions to the bottom line outside of the skylight. The rain screen principle (see Chapter 6) of pressure equalization should be followed in this scheme with special care. Also movement joints must be provided to accommodate framework movements.

10.3 Integration of PV modules

PV modules can be integrated into stick-system skylights either in the vision panels or in the spandrel area of the skylight, if it exists. The double-glazed units can be replaced by clear or opaque PV modules, preferably double-glazed. PV modules can be mounted and weatherproofed into the skylight in the same way as ordinary glass panels.

If PV modules are integrated into the vision area of the skylight, the module would form the outer lite of a clear double-glazed unit, equipped with low emissivity, solar control or high-performance coatings (Fig. 10.2). To avoid glass breakage due to thermal shock, the glass laminate would likely comprise heat-treated glazing. The build-up of the double glazed unit would also need to withstand structural actions such as wind loading, maintenance-imposed loads and meet safety requirements with regard to impact from building occupants. The inner pane of glass should be laminated to act as a safety line against free fall.

If PV modules are integrated into the spandrel area of the skylight, an opaque or semitransparent solar laminate could be used. The PV module could be integrated as a single- or double-glazed unit. The PV module would form the outer face of an insulated sandwich panel. If a double-glazed unit is chosen, coatings or ceramic fritting can be applied to one of the panes. The cavity behind the PV module would be drained, pressure equalised and fitted with an insulated panel finished off with an air and vapour seal. The heat build-up in the spandrel cavity or shadow box construction would require heat-treated glass to be used. A spandrel construction should be vapour-sealed and vented to the outside via the glazing rebate.

Fig. 10.2 Detail of a horizontal overhead glazing system with PV modules.

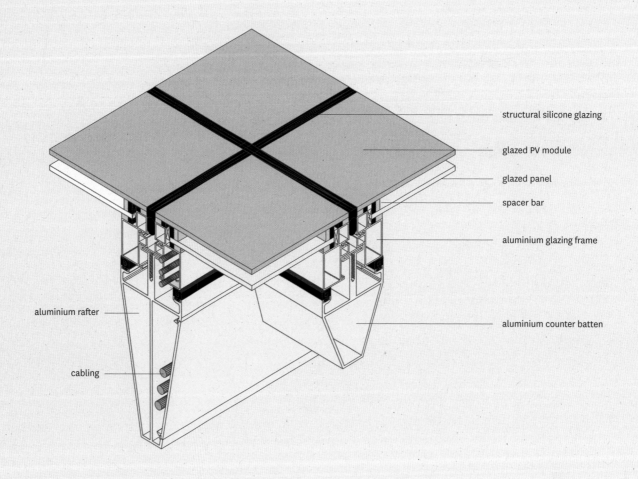

structural silicone glazing

glazed PV module

glazed panel

spacer bar

aluminium glazing frame

aluminium counter batten

aluminium rafter

cabling

Another possibility for integration would be to use hook-on or bolt-on PV modules forward of the spandrel area of the skylight after the system is constructed and made weathertight. If all conventional elements (such as glazing, insulation, seals) are in place, PV modules could be post-fixed to proprietary bracketry present in the spandrel area of the roof system. A drained, ventilated external cavity would space off the PV module from the insulated panel. The cavity would assure free cooling of the cells to maintain their efficiency.

Items that would require particular attention during design and detailing are:
— the location and integration of the junction box on the PV module
— the routing of electrical wiring along/through mullions and transoms
— the weather-tightness of perforations in the mullion and transom extrusions
— the junction box and the wiring exiting at edges of double-glazed units and the durability of the edge seals
— the ability of the PV module to take wind and maintenance loads

A combination of sunshade louvres as a superimposed system is a good solution for the integration of PV modules in to a skylight. The louvres can be movable to track the sun, and the intermediate space allows for ventilation and cooling of the modules.

10.4 Maintenance & replacement

Maintenance and replacement of a stick-system skylight with integrated PV modules will always occur from the outside. An important issue to consider when designing the building envelope is the replacement of glazing units and PV modules. Easy access to external and/or internal fixings and wiring needs to be carefully considered from the onset of the design.

If PV modules are integrated into the cladding system as glazing units, replacement would normally comprise demounting of gaskets, screws and pressure plates to release the infill panels from the framework and installation of the replacement unit. Replacement of such units means a temporary/partial removal of the weathering protection of the building envelope.

Access from the roof terrace around the skylight should be provided at the design stage, both for maintenance and for external cleaning. When deciding on a replacement strategy, the designer needs to also to consider the size and weight of the glazing units and PV modules. Access strategy and equipment should allow easy handling of larger components.

10.5 Case study: Nottingham University Jubilee Campus

Location

Town, country: Nottingham, UK
Latitude, longitude, elevation: 52.954°, –1.189°, 34 m
Average horizontal irradiation: 2.65 kWh/(m²·day)

PV

Area: 450 m²
Peak power specification: 53 kW$_p$
Power output: 51,240 kWh/y
Individual module dimensions:
1497 × 1170 mm
Technology: monocrystalline silicon
Manufacturer: BP Solar

Building

Type: business school
Height, storeys: 10 m, 3
Floor area: 1600 m²
Architects: Michael Hopkins & Partners
Completed: 1999

10.5.1 Background

The University of Nottingham located on University Park, the main campus, has always cultivated a reputation for promoting environmentally sustainable design. In the early 1990s with student numbers growing steadily, the University did not have space to expand. So in 1996 it held an architectural competition for a major development in a new location and with the aim of being a model of sustainable development for the region. The outcome of the competition was the creation of Jubilee Campus built on a site that previously had industrial use (**Fig. 10.3**).
One of the challenging aspects for design and construction of the first buildings on Jubilee Campus was the requirement to achieve an outstanding, innovative project in a short time period and within a tight budget. An application was made to the European Commission resulting in an EU Thermie (Technologies Européennes pour la Maîtrise de l'Energie) grant of £750,000. This supported development of the low-energy ventilation system which includes wind cowls in the form of 5 m high, aluminium-clad cones sitting on top of the air-handling units (**Fig. 10.4**). It also helped finance a PV system integrated into the sloping glass roofs of the full-height of the atria (**Fig. 10.6**).

Fig. 10.3 View onto west side of the Jubilee
Campus.
Photo: Paul McMullin
Courtesy: Arup

Fig. 10.4 The two inclined PV roofs of the School of Management and Finance, Jubilee Campus. In the background are wind cowls that form part of the natural ventilation system.
Photo: Paul McMullin
Courtesy: Arup

Fig. 10.5 PV roof panels showing the electrical connections.
Photo: Paul McMullin
Courtesy: Arup

Fig. 10.6 Atrium of the School of Management and Finance, Jubilee Campus, showing PV modules integrated into the central section of the roof.
Photo: Paul McMullin
Courtesy: Arup

10.5.2 PV system

The atrium roof is supported by laminated timber beams **(Fig. 10.5)**. The PV system uses pseudo square monocrystalline cells with 88 cells laminated into each glass-to-glass module. Clear spaces between the cells provide some transparency. The module dimensions are 1497×117 mm with 256 modules covering an area of $450\,m^2$. The total PV installation is rated at $53\,kW_P$ with an annual output of 51 MWh. The PV system is sized to meet the energy demands of the ventilation systems within the buildings when there is insufficient wind speed for the wind cowls.
As well as providing power for the ventilation fans, the PV modules provide shading for the atria. When the shading effect of the PV modules is significant and ambient light reduces, light sensors control artificial lighting for the atria to supplement natural light when necessary. There are no manually controlled light switches.

10.6 Case study: California Academy of Sciences

Town, country: San Francisco, USA
Latitude, longitude, elevation: 37.770°, −122.466°, 77 m
Average horizontal irradiation: 4.57 kWh/(m²·day)

Area: 920 m²
Peak power specification: 172 kW$_p$
Power output: 213,000 kWh/y
Individual module dimensions:
1046 × 1559 mm
Technology: monocrystalline silicon
Manufacturer: Sun Power Corp.

Type: museum
Height, storeys: 19 m, 5
Floor area: 38,000 m²
Architects: Renzo Piano
Completed: 2008

10.6.1 Background

In collaboration with architects Renzo Piano and Gordon H. Chong and Partners, Arup designed the California Academy of Sciences's new museum in San Francisco's Golden Gate Park (**Fig. 10.7**). The new Academy of Sciences building, which opened its doors to the public in 2008, includes an aquarium, planetarium, and natural history exhibits among other public spaces.

In keeping with the Academy's goals, the museum was designed to achieve high performance while minimizing environmental impacts and operational maintenance costs. Striving to achieve a Platinum LEED (Leadership in Energy and Environmental Design) rating, the building's sustainable features include a "green roof", natural ventilation, extensive use of natural daylight, reduced water run-off, alternative transportation, and integration into the park and community. BIPV is also a key part. Performance characteristics indicate that the new building will achieve significant benefits in terms of energy efficiency, reduction of stormwater runoff, minimization of heat-island effects and reduced biodiversity impacts.

Fig. 10.7 View from the north west of the California Academy of Sciences.
Photo courtesy: Arup

10.6.2 PV system

The main roof of the Academy is undulating in form and mostly covered with planting (Fig. 10.12). A flat canopy that extends around the full perimeter of the roof (Fig. 10.10) presented the best opportunity for integrating PV.

Monocrystalline silicon cells are laminated into bespoke glass-glass modules and used in a band of the canopy. The glass panes are each 1046 × 1559 × 8 mm and 77 PV cells make up a full module. The pattern of the opaque cells is copied in a friting pattern in the plain glass glazing on either side (Fig. 10.9).

The canopy contains 720 PV modules covering an area of 920 m² making it the largest PV glass canopy in the United States. The whole PV canopy was expected to generate nearly 213,000 kWh per year, supplying about 5% the Academy's electricity demand.

The structure of the canopy itself is made from recycled steel. It is attached to the main building with brackets (Fig. 10.7) and supported at strategic points by columns (Fig. 10.8 and Fig. 10.10). The plain glazing and PV modules are installed on top of the structure.

10.6.3 Sustainability features

In addition to the solar canopy, the Academy includes a number of technologies and materials which optimise heat and humidity, make the most of natural light and ventilation, maximise renewable energy sources and make efficient use water resources and recycled building materials.

For example, skylights on the green roof open and close automatically to vent hot air out when necessary (Fig. 10.11 and Fig. 10.12). There are motorised windows, which will automatically open and close to let cool air in. The lighting system includes photosensors which automatically dim the artificial lighting in response to ambient daylight penetration, thus minimising energy for interior illumination.

Fig. 10.8 Underside of the canopy showing the opaque PV cells and the vertical column support.
Photo: Cody Andreson

Fig. 10.9 Bracket connecting the structure of the canopy to the roof.
Photo courtesy: Arup

Fig. **10.10** PV canopy.
Photo courtesy: Arup

Fig. **10.11** Detail of an opened skylight.
Photo courtesy: Arup

Fig. **10.12** Green roof of the California Academy of Sciences showing skylights on one of the mounds.
Photo courtesy: Arup

10.7 Case study: Vauxhall Transport Interchange

Location

Town, country: London, UK
Latitude, longitude, elevation: 51.486°, −0.124°, 10 m
Average horizontal irradiation: 2.73 kWh/(m²·day)

PV

Area: 237 m²
Peak power specification: 30 kW$_P$
Power output: 23,760 kWh/y
Individual module dimensions: 1320 × 895 mm
Technology: hybrid monocrystalline & thin-film
amorphous silicon
Manufacturer: Sanyo

Building

Type: bus station
Height, storeys: 7 m, 1
Floor area: 2847 m²
Architects: Arup Associates
Completed: 2005

10.7.1 Background

Vauxhall Transport Interchange at Vauxhall Cross in south London is a busy transport hub but was in a run-down area previously notorious for its domination by traffic. Transport for London (TfL) wanted to create a coherent and efficient interchange for bus, rail and Underground users and indirectly to promote the use of public transport. Moreover TfL wanted a landmark structure to enhance the local environment and amenity. TfL commissioned a number of designs and the Office of the Mayor of London imposed two key objectives on the design:

— As a strategic transport centre, to promote use and accessibility of public transport with emphasis on walking and cycling and reduction in traffic congestion.
— In accordance with their Energy Strategy introduced in 2004, to reduce London's contribution to climate change, eradicate fuel poverty and promote and deliver sustainable energy for public transport.

Fig. 10.13 Undulating canopy of the Vauxhall Transport Interchange.
Photo: Christian Richters

Fig. 10.14 Hybrid PV modules on the cantilevers of the Vauxhall Transport Exchange.
Photo: Christian Richters

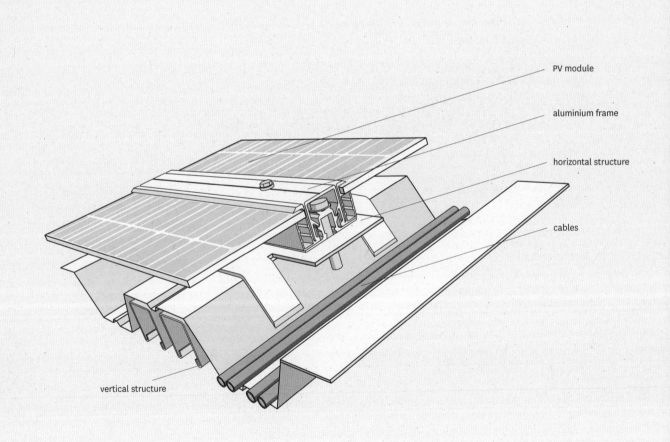

PV module

aluminium frame

horizontal structure

cables

vertical structure

Fig. 10.15 Fixing system of the PV modules to the Vauxhall Transport Interchange.

Fig. 10.16 Northern end of the Vauxhall Transport Interchange showing the integrated PV as seen from the ground.
Photo: Christian Richters

→ 10.7.1

The outcome includes a striking bus station as a symbol of regeneration, designed by architects Arup Associates. The bus station consists of a 200 m long, 12 m wide, undulating stainless-steel ribbon **(Fig. 10.13)**. The undulations along the length of the canopy reflect the frequency of bus stands. Each dip provides a seating refuge, which enhances and provides amenity for the local environment. The canopy rises over the height of a double-decker bus.

The principal intermodal circulation and the operational accommodation are at the canopy's northern end. The accommodation structure has been used as springing point to launch the ribbon's dramatic elevating twin cantilevers. These oversail the circulation area and underground access area. The upper surface of the cantilevers are clad with a PV array to generate supplementary power for the building.

10.7.2 PV system

Hybrid HIT technology was chosen for the PV modules for its high efficiency (see Chapter 2 for details). The technology combines ultra-thin amorphous silicon with monocrystalline silicon in one cell **(Fig. 10.14)**. In addition to high performance, the amorphous component makes effective use of diffused light from overcast skies.

The cantilevers are tilted at 20° from horizontal and just 5° west of south-facing. Because of the inclination, the PV cells are visible from the surrounding area, an important public demonstration of renewable energy use **(Fig. 10.16)**.

The modules are mounted over stainless-steel metal roof cladding fixed to the cantilever. The mounting method was designed by Arup to allow for flexing of the cantilevered canopy. The modules are held in a black anodized aluminium frame and mounted off the cladded roof using a slotted bolting system to the vertical rails **(Fig. 10.15)**.

Each of the canopy's forks carries four sub-arrays of 21 modules. These are connected in series strings to eight PV inverters mounted in the electrical plant room which provide a single phase output at 230 V, 50 Hz.

The 168 modules cover 237 m² of the upper surface of the long cantilevers. The measured annual output is almost 24 MWh per year, covering about 30% of the energy required to power the bus station.

10.8 Case study: Beijing Olympic Park

Town, country: Beijing, P.R. China
Latitude, longitude, elevation: 39.999°, 116.390°, 43 m
Average horizontal irradiation: 4.32 kWh/(m²·day)

Area: 341 m²
Power specification: 18 kW$_P$
Annual power output: 17,800 kWh/y
Individual module dimensions:
1000 × 415 to 857 mm
Technology: copper indium diselenide (CIS)
Manufacturer: Odersun

Type: multi-storey car park
Height, storeys: 8 m, 6
Floor area: 19,792 m²
Architects: Odersun
Completed: 2008

10.8.1 Background

This PV roof project was selected by the Beijing Olympic Organizing Committee (BOCOG) as a demonstration project of new solar energy technology. The PV application consists of four circular roofs as part of the underground parking of the visitors' centre of the Olympic Park in Beijing (**Fig. 10.17**). The roofs cover access ramps which spiral several storeys down into the parking levels.

The design of each roof consists of rings of trapezoidal panels in four concentric circles (**Fig. 10.18**). Each installation consists of 496 panels which are subdivided into four sectors of 124 panels each. The requirement was to cover the circular roof entirely with a PV array.

Fig. 10.17 View south onto three Odersun Solar Circles in the Olympic Park, with the Beijing Olympic Stadium in the background.
Photo: Arthur Thill
Courtesy: Odersun AG

Fig. 10.18 Arrangement of PV modules in each Odersun Solar Circle.

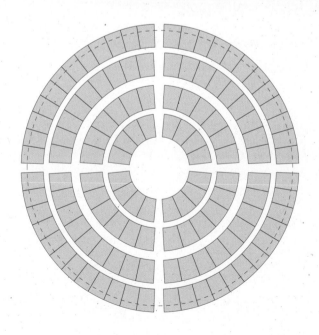

10.8.2 PV technology

The challenge of this BIPV project was to make trapezoidal PV modules. The technology of CIS manufactured by Odersun is suited to this bespoke requirement. Odersun specialise in applying CIS to a continuous copper-substrate strip 1 cm in width. Lengths of this strip are fabricated into a "supercell" of many strips connected in series. Connection is achieved by overlapping (Fig. 10.19). Supercells can be made in a range of dimensions. The length of the individual cell strips are simply cut from the roll and determine the current that can be drawn. The number of cells interconnected in series defines the voltage.

This technology allows great flexibility in terms of size and is thus suitable for trapezoidal modules. Each module trapezoidal requires three different supercell sizes. The four concentric rings mean there are four sizes of trapezoid, so for the whole project twelve different supercell sizes were produced.

The PV technology that has been used in these modules is the CIS-CuT, which consists in applying a non-silicon photovoltaic material on metal strips and interconnecting each strip by partial overlapping in order to obtain a supercell. The supercells can have different number of strips and different length, which influence the output of the module.

The PV system is installed on a horizontal steel structure supported by vertical H-beams, which are connected to cylindrical columns. These form the supporting structure for the access ramps to an underground parking lot. The columns were not roofed-over but are open at the top. These serve as exhaust ventilation shafts for the individual parking-lot storeys. This function must remain unimpaired after the PV system has been installed. For this reason, the PV systems, including the supporting sub-structures, had to be of an open design.

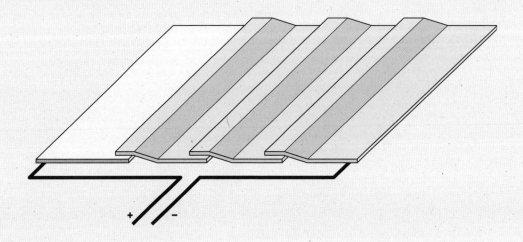

Fig. 10.19 Schematic of how CISCuT strip cells are joined in series by overlapping.

11. RESIDENTIAL

11.1 General

The residential sector can be divided into apartment blocks and low-rise housing. Apartment blocks have many similarities to the non-domestic sector, such as office buildings, which are covered by the range of BIPV systems in Chapters 5–10. This chapter contrasts the different façade requirements of the residential sector.
For low-rise traditional housing, the most applicable façade types for BIPV are roof systems and rainscreens.
A key difference of residential to other buildings for PV systems is closer attention to matching energy demand by use of the building to power generation by PV and other means. BIPV on a home is becoming one part of an overall energy strategy examining heating and electricity. As part of this approach, new-build residential is starting to incorporate solar aspects at the design stage in order to maximise solar performance where adjustments in orientation and form are possible.

11.2 Apartment blocks

For lightweight residential apartment blocks, there are similarities in form to commercial offices, as covered extensively in Chapters 5–10. A key difference however is that building regulations for domestic are generally stricter than for commercial build in that heat loss must be much lower. For lightweight construction, this means that demands on the façade are more challenging. Either curtain walling must have a low proportion of vision area or construction must be in non-curtain or traditional walling. Also, air permeability needs to be low whilst maintaining minimum levels of ventilation.
The options can be summarised in terms of the BIPV types (see Chapter 4, **Fig. 4.1**).
— Chapter 5: PV on shading devices is suitable but the area available is low and anyway the trend is to a low proportion of glazing in housing.
— Chapter 6: PV rainscreen applies to non-curtain and traditional walling.
— Chapter 7: stick-system needs to have a high performance.
— Chapter 8: unitised is relevant to high rise apartment blocks. It needs to have a high performance.
— Chapter 9: double-skin façade tends to be used for prestige offices and is not generally applicable to residential for its higher cost.
— Chapter 10: roofs are important areas to utilise, noting some of the principles in Chapter 3, **Fig. 3.10**.

11.3 Low-rise traditional houses

This group is characterised by traditional heavyweight or lightweight timber frame. The options can be summarised in terms of some of the BIPV types (see Chapter 4, **Fig. 4.1**:
— Rainscreen for vertical
— Roof, preferably sloping

PV systems for roofs are well developed. Standard modules are easy to lay on. Proprietary tiles are being introduced enabling simple integration to an increasing range of roof types (**Fig. 11.1**).

Fig. 11.1 PV integration into a pitched roof of a
low-rise traditional house.
Photo courtesy: Avancis

11.4 Case study: K2 apartments

Location

Town, country: Melbourne, Australia
Latitude, longitude, elevation: –37.852°, 144.983°, 19 m
Average horizontal irradiation: 4.1 kWh/(m²·day)

PV

Area: 268 m²
Peak power specification: 22 kW$_P$
Power output: 25,000 kWh/y
Individual module dimensions:
1000 × 2000 mm
Technology: monocrystalline silicon
Manufacturer: BP Solar

Building

Type: residential block
Height, storeys: 14, 17 & 25 m, 3, 4 & 7
Floor area: 4800 m²
Architects: DesignInc
Completed: 2007

11.4.1 Background

The K2 apartments are a medium-density, public housing development of 96 apartments, located in Windsor, a suburb of Melbourne, Australia (**Fig. 11.2**). K2 is the landmark ecologically sustainable development putting into practice the State Government of Victoria's approaches toward issues such as climate change and water scarcity.

The primary ecological objectives of the complex were to minimise greenhouse gas emissions and water consumption, to design for longevity and to use reusable and recycled materials.

The project embodies the integration of sustainable architecture at the conceptual stage of the design. Among the various environmentally sustainable design aspects there is a system for the grey-water treatment, and a careful choice of the building materials based on embodied energy, biodiversity, waste, end of life, reuse/recyclability, robustness and toxicity to human occupants, manufacturers and to the environment. The structural aspects follow passive solar design which guarantees high level of comfort both in summer and in winter. PV and solar collector systems are the active solar components.

The results are a comfortable indoor environment all year round and lower running costs than for traditionally designed units. It has won numerous awards.

Fig. 11.2 View from the north onto the K2 apartment development, Melbourne (AU).
Photo: Peter Hyatt
Courtesy: Arup

Fig. 11.3 Close-up of the PV installations in the foreground on the roof and pods. The roofs in the background have flat-plate solar water heaters.
Photographer: Peter Hyatt
Courtesy: Arup

11.4.2 PV technology

PV technology chosen was monocrystalline silicon for its high efficiency compared to polycrystalline and amorphous silicon technologies. The PV modules are located on some of the north-facing roofs and pod façades. The pod locations are tilted about 40° from the horizontal to optimise the power generation **(Fig. 11.3)**. Collectively the PV modules cover an area of 268 m², generating approximately 25,000 kWh per year.

The inverter equipment is positioned on the roof and integrated with the panel support structure.

11.4.3 Low-energy features

The potential of passive solar design has been utilised to the full, for example by optimising the building shape and orientation to enhance naturally ventilation which helps purging excess heat build up also in extreme conditions **(Fig. 11.4)**. Moreover the particular shape and orientation of the building excludes high-angle solar penetration during summer, thus reducing the risk of overheating. In winter double-glazed windows, exposed concrete ceilings, masonry walls and insulated construction help reduce the heat losses and provide thermal stability.

In addition to the PV arrays, solar hot-water collectors are installed on the north roof areas. They are sized to achieve at least 50% of the domestic hot-water demand. Energy-efficient lighting systems are used throughout, and energy-efficient lifts contribute to reduced overall energy use.

In order to monitor the performance of the building and its components and to increase the awareness of the occupants towards the sustainable measures installed in the complex, each apartment is equipped with energy meters.

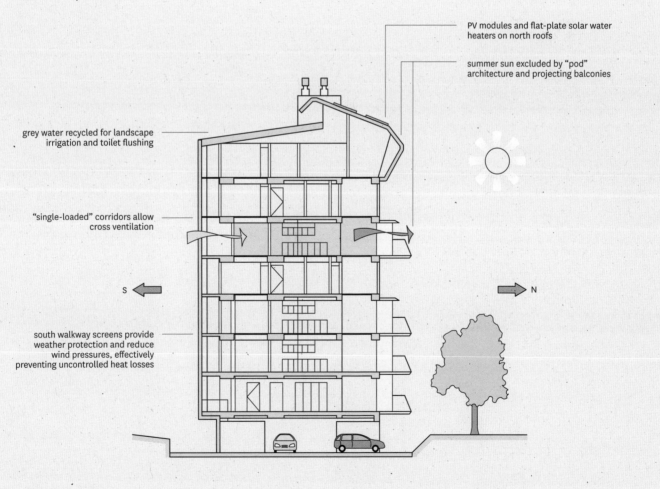

Fig. 11.4 Schematic of some of the low-energy features on the K2 apartments.

PV modules and flat-plate solar water heaters on north roofs

summer sun excluded by "pod" architecture and projecting balconies

grey water recycled for landscape irrigation and toilet flushing

"single-loaded" corridors allow cross ventilation

S

N

south walkway screens provide weather protection and reduce wind pressures, effectively preventing uncontrolled heat losses

11.5 Case study: Upton ZED terrace

Town, country: Northampton, UK
Latitude, longitude, elevation: 52.232°, –0.942°, 70 m
Average horizontal irradiation: 2.7 kWh/(m²·day)

PV

Area: 157 m²
Peak power specification: 22 kW$_P$
Power output: 16,230 kWh/y estimated
Individual module dimensions:
1318 × 994 mm
Technology: monocrystalline silicon
Manufacturer: Sharp

Building

Type: residential housing
Height, storeys: 8 m, 2
Floor area: 602 m² (6 houses)
Architects: ZEDfactory
Completed: 2009

11.5.1 Background

Upton is an urban extension for Northampton with the client, Metropolitan Housing Partnership, acting both as developer and social-housing provider. First dwellings became available in 2007. The development is in association with English Partnerships who stipulated high quality sustainable specifications. The overall project is a national example of best practice in sustainable urban growth and a model for the design of other urban extensions across the country. The buildings achieve low-energy thermal performance utilising high levels of thermal insulation, high levels of air-tightness with heat-recovery ventilation and various types of renewable energy technologies.

Partway through construction in 2007, the UK Government introduced the Code for Sustainable Homes. The highest level in the code's rating system, level 6, significantly raises the standard of the environmental performance of residential buildings. A level-6 house design must be net-zero carbon, including the energy required for space and water heating and all the electrical power demands of the home. It represents a new international industry standard for low environmental impact zero carbon living. The UK Government intention is that by 2016, all new homes in the UK will be built to these standards.

Fig. 11.5 View of the south façade of the Upton ZED terrace.
Photo: www.ruralzed.com
Courtesy: ZEDfactory Ltd.

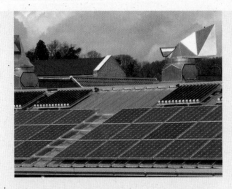

Fig. 11.6 Close-up of the south roof of the Upton ZED terrace showing a ventilation cowl (in the north roof), solar thermal panels near the roof ridge and the PV array lower downt. The horizontal support rails for the PV modules are visible between two parts of the PV array.
Photo: www.ruralzed.com
Courtesy: ZEDfactory Ltd.

Fig. 11.7 Detail of the PV module attachment system showing how the support rail interfaces with the standing seam.
Photo: www.ruralzed.com
Courtesy: ZEDfactory Ltd.

Fig. 11.8 View from southeast of development showing the terrace of 6 houses in the foreground.
Rendering courtesy: Franklin Ellis Architects

→ 11.5.1

Within the Upton development, a terrace of six houses by the architects ZEDfactory had been conceived to very high thermal performance (**Fig. 11.5** and **Fig. 11.8**). They are referred to as solar "ZED" (standing for zero [fossil] energy development) because they maximise solar gain on the south side and use thermal mass within that operates as a heat sink to store solar heat gains. The ZED terrace was selected for further development to meet the full level 6 carbon-neutral specification to achieve a "true zero-carbon" dwelling.

11.5.2 Energy provision

The ZED terrace is south-facing. South-facing homes have lower winter fuel consumption than east west-facing units. High-performance windows ensure that large areas of glazing can be used to give excellent daylight and good solar gain (**Fig. 11.5**). There is extendable shading on south-facing windows to prevent summer overheating. There are high standards for measures of airtight, super-insulated building fabric, with heat recovery ventilation. To ensure adequate ventilation without parasitic energy penalty of electric fans, the terrace features wind-driven ventilation cowls with heat recovery (**Fig. 11.6** and **Fig. 11.9**).

Biomass and solar thermal panels provide 100% of the domestic hot water requirement whilst passive solar gain through controllable south-facing sunspaces provides nearly all the space heating with biomass fuelled heating as a backup only. Together with 32 other dwellings, the six properties within the Code 6 ZED Terrace are served by the wood pellet district heating system in the development from a central boiler house. Solar thermal panels use the efficient evacuated tube type collector. The capacity was limited to two panels per dwelling to free up the south-facing roof space for electricity generating PV modules.

To achieve code level 6, low and zero carbon (LZC) technologies must be used to offset the cooking, lighting and appliances electricity consumption.

PV was chosen as the principle electricity generator. PV is referred to as offset since electricity is drawn from the grid when needed, while these renewables export to the grid according to conditions for generation (sun shining). An energy balance between import and export is achieved over a twelve-month period.

The ZED terrace is also intended to showcase renewable technologies. Therefore, whilst a PV only installation would be the cost-effective solution, some of the houses in ZED terrace also utilise a micro-wind turbine.

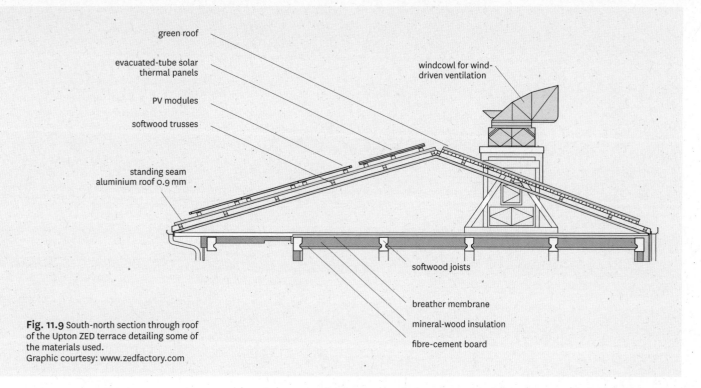

Fig. 11.9 South-north section through roof of the Upton ZED terrace detailing some of the materials used.
Graphic courtesy: www.zedfactory.com

The micro-wind turbine technology is a Swift upwind horizontal axis rated at 1.5 kW at a rated wind speed of 12.5 m/s. The rotor is 5-blade of diameter 2.12 m. Peak output is between 13 m/s and 20 m/s wind speed and it is estimated that one wind turbine will generate about 500 kWh/y.

11.5.3 PV technology

The dwellings are three-bedroom houses of 100 m², using low-energy appliances and low-energy lighting. The electrical requirement is calculated as 3208 kWh/y from lighting, appliances and cooking. This is equivalent to emissions of 1354 kg CO_2/y using the grid-supplied factor for the UK of 0.422 kg CO_2/kWh.

To maximise south-facing roof area for PV, the design was slightly modified to move the pitch beyond the terrace centre line (**Fig. 11.9**). Monocrystalline silicon was selected with 180 W_p modules. Twenty modules gives a 3.6 k W_p array per dwelling. Insolation values were available from the BRE SAP calculator of 933 kWh/(m²·y) at tilt angle 0° and 1042 kWh/(m²·y) at tilt angle 30°. The array is at 19° so a weighted average of 1002 kWh/(m²·y) was used. This gives a predicted electrical output of 2705 kWh/y. Since this generation is embedded, the conversion factor to CO_2 emissions is called "grid displaced" and takes into account avoidance of long-distance transmissions losses. The factor is 0.568 kg CO_2/kWh, so the emissions reduction is 1536 kg CO_2/y. This is higher than the 1354 kg CO_2/y for grid-supplied electricity so the house will be carbon-neutral as required.

The modules use a simple frame connection to the standing seam aluminium roof (**Fig. 11.6** and **11.7**). A 50 mm air space enables ventilation to ameliorate peak temperature, while giving a uniform appearance.

12.
REFURBISHMENT

12.1 Refurbishment situations

There are a variety of refurbishment situations in which the opportunity to integrate PV could be considered:
— Failure in the façade or roof that requires intervention.
— Need to improve the façade or roof performance.
— To make the building more attractive to tenants.

Related to refurbishment could be adding PV to a building that can not be demolished, such as one of historic value or in a conservation area. In a conservation area, it is the street face that is most likely to be protected, so façade retention may be a solution.
The challenge for integrating PV in refurbishment is working within the constraints of the existing structure and local planning regulation. For heritage buildings, there may be the additional constraints of agreeing detail with conservation officers.

12.2 BIPV opportunities

For considering BIPV opportunities, building types can be divided into curtain wall and traditional build (see Chapter 4).
When a building with a curtain wall is refurbished, this generally means that the fabric is stripped back to the floor plate and vertical support columns. Although the overall project might be referred to as a refurbishment, the replacement curtain wall is likely to be new. Therefore Chapter 7 on the stick system and Chapter 8 on the unitised system apply with no special comments needed here.
For an older or historic building, sometimes an outer glazed skin enables the original walls to be left intact and visible while the new outer skin provides protection, although this is relatively unusual. This constitutes a new double-skin façade, as covered in Chapter 9.
Traditional build (as described in Chapter 4) has the best opportunities for incorporating BIPV as part of refurbishment. Integration is most often incorporated in the rainscreen. The case study in this chapter is for a rainscreen and shows use of standard modules within the constraints of the existing window lines of the building.
Reference can also be made to the two case studies in Chapter 6 which covers rainscreens in detail. In fact the two case studies in that chapter are both on existing buildings. The new rainscreen in case study 6.5 was in response to a façade failure. The rainscreen in case study 6.6 was to improve a previously rather plain façade. However in both cases the façades covered large plain areas with few spatial constraints. They had almost as much freedom of design as if the buildings were new, hence their inclusion in that chapter rather than here.

12.3 Case study: Northumberland Building

Location

Town, country: Newcastle upon Tyne, UK
Latitude, longitude, elevation: 54.978°, –1.608°, 51 m
Average horizontal irradiation: 2.6 kWh/(m²·day)

PV

Area: 430 m²
Peak power specification: 40 kW$_P$
Power output: 25,000 kWh/y
Individual module dimensions:
1180 × 520 mm
Technology: monocrystalline silicon
Manufacturer: BP Solar
Completed: 1994

Building

Type: services, psychology & sport sciences
Height, storeys: 18 m, 4
Floor area: 4700 m²
Architects: Ove Arup & Partners

12.3.1 Background

In 1991 a report funded by the UK Government Department of Trade and Industry into the potential of BIPV for a commercial building showed that PV could be made into a cladding component. Furthermore its power match was ideal for commercial building applications. A building was needed on which to demonstrate these findings.

One of the report's authors was the Newcastle Photovoltaic Applications Centre at the University of Northumbria. The University had a concrete framed building with precast concrete cladding units which needed refurbishing (**Fig. 12.1**). The building is typical of 1960s construction for which the cladding has provided protection for over twenty years before refurbishment is required. It is rectangular in plane, four storeys and with the main elevations facing approximately north and south. The concrete cladding incorporating a mosaic finish was suffering from carbonation, reinforcement corrosion and mosaic detachment. The entire cladding and window frames had to be removed.

This provided an ideal base on which to demonstrate photovoltaic building integration. However while the University had the money for the cladding replacement, it could not fund the additional cost of the photovoltaic integration. Eventually the necessary finance was provided by private and public sources: 40% from a European Community Thermie Grant, 9% from ETSU in the UK and 51% from private-sector sponsors.

Fig. 12.1 View onto the southwest corner of North-umberland Building before refurbishment.
Photo courtesy: Arup

Fig. 12.2 South elevation of the Northumberland Building showing the PV cladding inclined 25° from vertical between the windows.
Photo courtesy: Arup

Fig. 12.3 Framework for one cladding unit that holds five standard PV modules.
Photo courtesy: Arup

Fig. 12.4 Hook-system retaining framework holding the PV modules in place.
Photo courtesy: Arup

12.3.2 Cladding design

The PV cladding design followed the principle of rainscreen cladding which provides a building with protection from the elements but with a ventilated space between the cladding and the building to equalise wind pressure and prevent condensation. The design of the cladding to the south face included photovoltaics while on the north face a traditional aluminium rainscreen was used.

In order to provide better solar collection, particularly from the low winter sun, the cladding on the south side was inclined at 25° from vertical (**Fig. 12.2**, **Fig. 12.5** and **Fig. 12.6**). Another benefit of this approach is that the overhang provides at the head of the window below some shading to reduce summertime solar gain in the building. Also the inclined design gives the building a better aesthetic.

Standard BP Saturn modules were used with dimensions of 1180 × 520 mm and a nominal rating of 85 W$_p$. Five of these modules were assembled into a cladding unit which consisted of a 3 mm aluminium powder coated framework (**Fig. 12.3**). The width of each cladding unit conveniently aligned with four window units.

The cladding units were designed to be manufactured off site and fitted to the façade on an aluminium framework bolted to the building (**Fig. 12.4**). The inclined design provided space behind both for ventilation which assists in controlling module temperature and for the wiring trunking, junction boxes and monitoring equipment.

The cladding design allowed for each cladding unit to be individually supported and with a separate wiring connection. Therefore should a unit be damaged or need repair the whole system would not be affected while the work was undertaken.

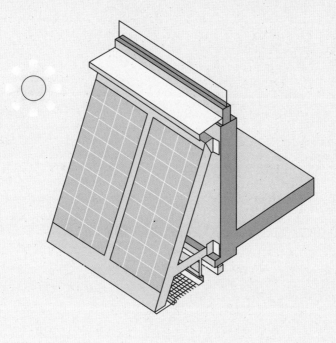

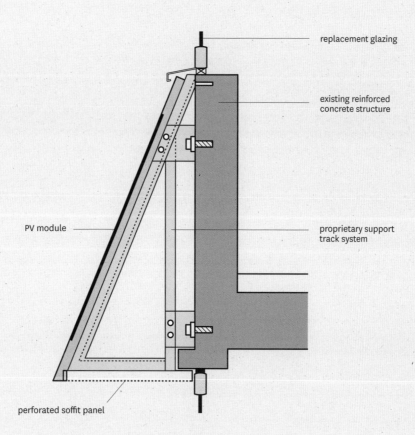

replacement glazing

existing reinforced
concrete structure

PV module

proprietary support
track system

perforated soffit panel

Fig. 12.5 Schematic of 2 PV modules in the inclined
façade.

Fig. 12.6 Vertical section through support system.

12.3.3 Wiring design

Each string of fifteen laminates is connected in series to give a nominal operating voltage of 270 V at the maximum power point. The output of the 31 strings is fed into a line commutated, thyrister inverter with a power rating of 40 kW. This converts the DC input to a 415 V, 3-phase AC output which is comparable with the conventional power supply to the building. The inverter, manufactured and supplied by SMA GmbH, incorporates maximum power-point tracking. It complies with local regional electricity company regulations (G-5911) including automatic shutdown of the inverter if the grid supply voltage or frequency varies beyond defined limits, although a relaxation of the cut-off protection from 0.5 to 2 seconds was allowed The inverter is designed for maximum efficiency at 25% load but compensation circuits allow it to retain a relatively high efficiency throughout the load curve.

The DC switch panel incorporates line and load circuit breakers for each string, blocking diodes for protection of shaded strings, current and voltage monitoring devices and terminals for measurement of string I-V characteristics. The line circuit breaker provides compliance with Health and Safety regulations, which demand that a circuit breaker is located as close as possible to the power source (in this case the PV string). The load circuit breaker allows investigation of any single string without closing down the entire system. The five PV modules in each cladding unit were fully wired in the factory in order to speed up erection on site.

12.3.4 Installation

Work on the building commenced in June 1994 with the removal of the old cladding and replacement of the windows. Additional insulation was fixed to the concrete upstand walls with the PV electrical installation commencing in September 1994 comprising the fixing of junction boxes and wiring to the inverter room.
The photovoltaic cladding units were hung in October and wired into the junction boxes. The installation was completed on a level-by-level basis commencing at the top followed by stripping down the scaffold.
As the photovoltaic modules produce electricity as soon as they are exposed to the light, the modules were covered with a black plastic film when being assembled. This film remained in place until the cladding units were installed and fully wired up.

12.3.5 Performance

The performance matched original predictions with the highest DC output of 40 kW. The output from the 465 PV modules provides around 30% of the average electrical building load. At weekends some power has been exported for use by other buildings on the University Campus.
The average performance ratio over 1995/96 was 0.609. An unshaded array may expect a performance ratio of 0.75–0.85 but, because of shading, highest value achieved was 0.659.
Because this was a demonstration project and the first large-scale integration of PV modules into the façade of a commercial building, all involved with the design and installation were on a learning curve.

13. CASE STUDY PERFORMANCE DATA

13.1 General

This handbook includes fourteen case studies, as selected to illustrate a range of BIPV approaches. They also provide a set of real data on working systems from around the world with full installation details. In this chapter the annual specific yield and annual area yield are calculated for each case study to compare their output performance.

13.2 Annual specific yield

Chapter 3 lists some of the factors that determine power output. Actual measured output from completed projects is an important resource from which to compared predicted output from new installations in similar conditions.

Specific yield is an important parameter that is calculated and listed here. Annual specific yield is "the amount of energy [kWh] produced over one year by a specific quantity of installed PV modules [$1\,kW_P$]". Note that the measure is independent of the type of solar technology used. The values from the case studies range from under $500\,kWh/(kW_P{\cdot}y)$ to over $1000\,kWh/(kW_P{\cdot}y)$.
Factors that affect the specific yield:
— Latitude
   This determines the sun path for the location and gives a rough indication of overall solar power available. For a low latitude (near the Equator), the sun passes high over at midday so a low tilt angle is best and insolation values are generally high.
— Insolation
   This is a meteorological measurement. It is affected by both the latitude and local weather conditions.
— Tilt
   This is a feature of the type of integration, whether on a vertical 90° façade, a horizontal 0° roof or at some angle in between on a sloped facet. For the maximum annual output, the tilt is generally set about equal 20° less than the latitude angle.
— Orientation
   This is a feature of the type of integration where the PV array is tilted from horizontal. For the maximum annual output, the orientation is generally set between southwest and southeast for the northern hemisphere, and between northwest and northeast for the southern hemisphere.

Specific yield is also affected by other factors, such as whether there is any shading, quality of wiring and performance of the inverter.

13.3 Annual area yield

From the specific yield, the amount of area needed is determined by the type of PV technology and whether the cells are well packed in a module or spaced for transparency.

13.4 Using the table

The following table aims to give some guidance on the electrical output to be expected from a BIPV system based on the performance of the case studies. Since the latitude of a project has a major affect on output, the case studies are listed in order of decreasing latitude, from Newcastle (UK) at 55° to McKinney (USA) at 33°.

When using the table for a new project of interest, first identify those rows near the latitude of your project. Use the annual specific yield in these rows to show the output that might be expected for each kW$_P$ of your PV array. Alternatively for a given area available on a building for a PV array, use the annual area yield, but note that this varies with technology of PV.

When using either the specific or area yield values from the table, use the other details given in table to indicate whether output from your project might be higher or lower:

— If the insolation of your site is known, it can be compared to the range of insolation values in the table at your latitude of interest. Otherwise check the map of insolation around the world in **Fig. 3.20**.

— Note dependence on tilt and orientation. **Fig. 3.5** and **3.6** gives an indication of how different facets of a building can be compared.

Section reference	Latitude (positive for northern hemisphere, negative for southern hemisphere)	Country, city	Annual average of horizontal insolation [kWh/m²·d]	Tilt from horizontal; orientation (hor.): horizontal so orientation does not apply	Annual specific yield [kWh/(kW$_P$·y)]	Technology (see Chapter 2)	Annual area yield [kWh/(m²·y)]	Peak power specification, area.	Annual PV output [kWh/y]	Case study
12.2	55°	UK, Newcastle	2.62	65° S	633	mcs	58	40 kW$_P$, 430 m²	25,000	Northumberland Building
7.7	54°	Germany, Hamburg	2.73	90° S	599	pcs	60	18 kW$_P$, 179 m²	10,800	Tobias Grau Head office
6.5	53°	UK, Manchester	2.53	90° NW-SE	468	pcs	46	391 kW$_P$, 3972 m²	183,000	The Co-operative Insurance Tower
10.5	53°	UK, Nottingham	2.65	0° (hor.)	967	mcs	114	53 kW$_P$, 450 m²	51,240	Jubilee Campus
11.5	52°	UK, Upton	2.74	19° S	751*	mcs	103*	22 kW$_P$, 157 m²	16,230*	Upton ZED terrace
10.7	51°	UK, London	2.73	20° S	792	HIT	100	30 kW$_P$, 237 m²	23,760	Vauxhall Transport Interchange
5.5	44°	Italy, Faenza	3.82	70° SW-NE	1482*	mcs	117*	23 kW$_P$, 285 m²	33,345*	Galleria Naviglio
9.4	42°	Spain, Mataró	4.31	90° S	995	pcs	93	20 kW$_P$, 255 m²	20,000	Pompeu Fabra Library
10.8	40°	P.R. China, Beijing	4.32	6° all directions	989*	CIS	52*	18 kW$_P$, 341 m²	17,800*	Beijing Olympic Park
6.6	40°	P.R. China, Beijing	4.32	90° E	492	pcs	73	79 kW$_P$, 534 m²	38,929	Xicui Entertainment Complex
11.4	−38°	Australia, Melbourne	4.12	25°, 40° N	1136	mcs	93	22 kW$_P$, 268 m²	25,000	K2 Apartments
8.6	−38°	Australia, Melbourne	4.12	70°, 74° N	870	pcs	94	46 kW$_P$, 426 m²	40,000	Alan Gilbert Building
10.6	38°	USA, San Francisco	4.57	0° (hor.)	1238	mcs	232	172 kW$_P$, 920 m²	213,000	California Academy of Sciences
8.7	33°	USA, McKinney	4.54	90° S	734*	mcs	82*	32 kW$_P$, 287 m²	23,500*	Wal-Mart Experimental Supercenter
					800*	tfas	89*	3 kW$_P$, 27 m²	2400*	

* predicted since no measured data available

CIS: copper indium diselenide
HIT: hybrid mcs and tfas
mcs: monocrystalline silicon
pcs: polycrystalline silicon
tfas: thin-film amorphous silicon

14. GLOSSARY OF TERMS AND INDEX

A

Air-mass number

A measure used to define the spectral distribution of sunlight for the illumination equipment used to test modules. It represents the path length of sunlight through the atmosphere and is expressed in comparison with unit path length where the sun is directly overhead (only possible for latitudes between the Tropic of Cancer and the Tropic of Capricorn).

Air-Mass 1.5 (AM 1.5)

The air-mass number where the path of sunlight through the atmosphere is 50% longer than when the sun is directly overhead. The sun's direction is 48° from the overhead position, as relevant for latitudes outside of the Tropics.

Alternating current (AC)

Electric current in which the direction of flow is reversed continuously. The conventional grid supply is AC at 60 Hz in Europe and 50 Hz in North America.

Amorphous

The microscopic physical state of a solid in which the atoms are not arranged in the orderly pattern of the crystalline form.

Awnings

Covering to screen persons or parts of buildings from the sun or rain.

B

Balance of system (BOS)

The parts of a PV system other than the PV array itself, for example support structure, wiring, isolators and invertors.

Building envelope

The outside of a building that contains the interior space, including the roof, the skin or waterproof covering of the structure.

Bypass diode

A bypass diode is connected in parallel across a part of the solar cells of a PV module. It protects these solar cells from thermal destruction in case of total or partial shading of individual solar cells whilst other cells are exposed to full light. It is connected in reverse to the polarity of the module so that it only conducts when the module is shaded.

C

Cladding panel

A generic term for an element which provides a "skin" to the building. It may attach directly to the building superstructure or may be supported off a secondary frame of mullions and transoms.

Conversion efficiency

The ratio of the electrical energy produced by a PV cell (or module) to the energy from sunlight incident on the cell (or module). This is usually quoted under standard test conditions (STC).

Crystalline

The microscopic physical state of a solid where the atoms are arranged in an ordered pattern.

Curtain wall

A system of lightweight wall construction usually comprising transparent and opaque panels supported on an aluminium frame which carry no vertical loads other than those due to its self-weight and any equipment attached to it and no horizontal loads other than those due to wind, maintenance and occupancy.

D

Dead load

Load due to the weight of all walls, permanent partitions, roofs, floors and all other permanent construction.

Diffuse radiation

Solar radiation scattered by the atmosphere, particularly clouds.

Direct current (DC)

Electric current which flows in one direction from the positive terminal of an illuminated PV module through electric loads to the negative terminal.

Direct radiation

Solar radiation transmitted directly through the atmosphere.

Diode

An electronic component that conducts electricity in one direction only.

E

Electron

Negatively charged atomic particle. An electric current is the movement of electrons through a material, such as a metal or semiconductor.

EVA

A common encapsulation medium for cells in PV modules. It is cross-linkable ethylene vinyl acetate.

G

Gasket

A preformed elastic seal used between joints of different components. Often used to accommodate tolerance or movement whilst also providing a barrier against wind and rain.

Global irradiance

The total irradiance (sunlight intensity) falling on a surface, this being the sum of the direct and diffuse irradiance.

Grid (on a PV cell)

The patterned metal contact on the top of the PV cell.

I

Inverter

A PV inverter is a power converter which transforms DC voltage and current from PV modules into single or multiphase AC voltage and current. A grid-connected inverter is designed to convert energy only when the mains grid is available.

Irradiance

The instantaneous intensity of solar radiation on a surface (W/m^2).

Irradiation

The cumulative amount of solar energy received on a surface (kWh/m^2).

Insolation

Incoming solar radiation measured at given location and a given tilt angle.

L

Live load

Variable load produced by the intended occupancy or use (people, furniture, electrical appliances). Wind load is not included in the live load.

Load (electric)

Any device or appliance (or set of devices or appliances) which uses electrical power. This contrasts with "live load" which relates to forces exerted on structural members.

Low-emissivity glass

Glass with a low-emissivity coating on one surface. This allows short-wavelength energy from the sun to pass through but reflects long-wavelength energy back in.

Low-iron glass

"White" glass providing high transparency.

M

Maximum power-point tracker (MPPT)

Part of a PV inverter which functions as an optimal electrical load for PV modules.

Monocrystalline silicon

Silicon for a PV cell that has a single and continuous crystal lattice structure with almost no defects or impurities. "Single" is used interchangeably with the prefix "mono".

Multi-junction cells

Two or more different cells with more than one p-n junction. Such an arrangement allows a greater portion of the sun's spectrum to be converted to electricity.

N

Nominal array power

The power rating of a PV array in W_p, as measured under standard test conditions (STC).

P

p-n junction

A zone in a piece of semiconductor material formed by different doping types. This is the usual configuration for a PV cell.

Parallel connection

A method of interconnecting two or more electricity producing or power-using devices, such that the voltage produced is not increased. However the current is additive. This is opposite to series connection.

Photovoltaic (PV) cell

A semiconductor device that converts light to electricity using the photovoltaic effect.

Polycrystalline silicon

Silicon that has solidified at such a rate that many small crystals (crystallites) are formed. The atoms within a single crystallite are symmetrically arranged, whereas the crystallites are jumbled together. "Multi" is used interchangeably with the prefix "poly".

Pressure-equalised

The technique of equalising pressure across different cavities in the build-up of façade to avoid rainwater being driven by kinetic energy through the façade.

PV module

A collection of interconnected PV cells encapsulated between protective materials (glass, polymers etc), sometimes mounted in an aluminium frame.

R

Rainscreen

A relatively cheap, open-jointed cladding system that is erected on rails on a waterproofed blockwork wall, or similar.

S

Series connection

A method of interconnecting devices that generate or use electricity so that the voltage is additive. The same current passes through each part of the circuit. This is the opposite of parallel connection.

Solar-selective glass

Glass with a solar-selective coating on one surface. This allows the visible spectrum of the radiation to pass through the glass and to reflect part of the long wavelength outward.

Spandrel

A type of cladding panel which occurs at floor level to hide the building superstructure, raised floor and false ceiling. It provides insulation and a smoke stop zone.

Standard test conditions (STC)

Standard test conditions are defined as an irradiance of $1000\,W/m^2$ at normal incidence, a spectral distribution of that irradiance equivalent to AM1.5 and a cell temperature of 25°C.

Stand-alone (PV system)

An autonomous or hybrid photovoltaic system not connected to a grid. Most stand-alone systems require batteries or some other form of electricity storage.

Stick system

A type of curtain walling where individual mullions and transoms are assembled on site to form a secondary frame to which cladding panels are attached.

String

A number of PV modules connected together electrically in series.

Structural glazing

A system of retaining glass or other materials to the aluminium members of a curtain wall using silicon sealant. These systems use no mechanical fasteners, and as a result have no profiles casting shadows on the glazing surface.

System yield

Useful energy supplied to the load by the PV system, which is expressed as a function of the nominal array power (kWh per kW_P) and over one year.

T

Tedlar

Dupont trade name for a film of polyvinyl fluoride (PVF). A commonly used laminate for the back surface of PV modules.

U

Unitised system

A type of curtain walling where mullions, transoms and cladding panels are factory-assembled into units, often 1.5m wide by a storey height, before delivery to site.

W

Watt (W)

Unit of power. Check context because it can refer to light energy with irradiance or electrical energy.

Watt-hour (Wh)

Unity of energy; one Wh is consumed when one watt of power is used for a period of one hour.

Watt peak (W_P)

Power output of a PV module under standard test conditions.

Index

Acknowledgements

The first concept for this book was a façade engineering design guide by Pieter Mattelaer in 2003 for internal use at Arup. This was later developed in 2005 in an architect's guide by Ignacio Fernandez as part of a collaborative research programme, "Improved Building Integration of PV by using Thin Film Modules in CIS Technology". We are grateful for funding of that research under the EU's Sixth Framework Programme, Priority 6.1 "Sustainable Energy Systems". Also our thanks go to Dieter Geyer and EU colleagues in the research consortium.

In bringing these earlier works up to date, we are indebted to contributions from and review by colleagues both at Arup and from other organisations. Particular thanks on technical input go to Edith Mueller, Graham Dodd, Rick Wheal, Chris Jofeh, Deborah Lazarus, Harris Poirazis and Professor David Infield. We are very grateful for critique of the text by Richard Hough, Colin Axon, Professor John Twidell, Ann Marie Aguilar, David Seager, Malcolm Ball, Jacob Dunn and Antony Rix. Also our thanks to Laurent Ngoc in the Arup Berlin office for his commitment to technical accuracy in the German version.

We wish to record our appreciation to project directors and others who have enabled us to describe the case studies as accurately as possible. Any omissions or inaccuracies are our fault. Thanks go to Keith Rudd, Natalie Drew, Alisdair McGregor, John King, Steve Walker, Schaun Landman, Carlos Prada, Nick Adams, Cody Andersen, Korinna Penndorf, David Fletcher, Keith Morrison and Pagani Paola.

For coordinating all the photographs, we are indebted to Flora Tonking and staff in the Arup Photo Library, particularly Pauline Shirley and Joanne Johnstone. Deborah Bird and Angela Bennett were very helpful with sourcing images, and we extend our appreciation to the many photographers who have allowed their work to be used. Conversion of our sketches into quality graphics owes to the dedication of Phil Bogan, Sam Wai, Sean Mcdermott and Daniel Blackhall. Additional help has been provided by Rebecca Roberts and Jenny Bonwick, and financial support was provided by the Arup Design and Technical Fund.

Finally we are very grateful to Ulrike Ruh, Nadine Rinderer, Alexander Felix and Jan K. Knapp of Birkhäuser for their imagination and dedication to converting our work into this book with such care.

Authors: Simon Roberts, Nicolò Guariento
Editorial collaboration: Alexander Felix, Jan K. Knapp
Picture editors: Flora Tonking, Jan K. Knapp

Cover: The Xicui Entertainment Complex, Beijing, part way through installation of the PV and LED facade.
Photo: Frank P. Palmer
Courtesy: Simone Giostra & Partners/Arup

Layout and cover design: Nadine Rinderer
Typesetting: Nadine Rinderer, Amelie Solbrig

The technical recommendations contained in this book reflect the current state of technology. However, they expressly require to be checked explicitly against current valid laws, regulations and standards of the country in question by the specialist planning bodies responsible. Author and publishing house can under no circumstances be held liable for the design, planning or execution of faulty structures.

Library of Congress Control Number: 2009924919

This book is also available in a German language edition:
ISBN 978-3-7643-9949-8

Bibliographic information published by the German National Library
The German National Library lists this publication in the Deutsche Nationalbibliografie; detailed bibliographic data are available on the Internet at http://dnb.d-nb.de.

© 2009 Birkhäuser Verlag AG
Basel · Boston · Berlin
P.O. Box 133, CH-4010 Basel, Switzerland
Part of Springer Science+Business Media

ARUP

Printed on 100% recycled paper.
Printed in Germany

ISBN: 978-3-7643-9948-1

9 8 7 6 5 4 3 2 1   www.birkhauser.ch